INSIDE THE LINES

"You must accept my word."

INSIDE THE LINES

By
EARL DERR BIGGERS
AND
ROBERT WELLES RITCHIE

Founded on Earl Derr Biggers'
Play of the Same Name

WILDSIDE PRESS: MMIII

Published by:
Wildside Press, LLC
P.O. Box 301
Holicong, PA 18928-0301 USA
www.wildsidepress.com

First Wildside edition: 2003

CONTENTS

INSIDE THE LINES

INSIDE THE LINES

CHAPTER I

JANE GERSON, BUYER

"**I** HAD two trunks—two, you ninny! Two! *Ou est l'autre?*"

The grinning customs guard lifted his shoulders to his ears and spread out his palms. "*Mais, mamselle——*"

"Don't you '*mais*' me, sir! I had two trunks —*deux troncs*—when I got aboard that wabbly old boat at Dover this morning, and I'm not going to budge from this wharf until I find the other one. Where *did* you learn your French, anyway? Can't you understand when I speak your language?"

The girl plumped herself down on top of the unhasped trunk and folded her arms truculently. With a quizzical smile, the customs guard looked down into her brown eyes, smold-

1

ering dangerously now, and began all over
again his speech of explanation.

"*Wagón-lit?*" She caught a familiar word.
"*Mais oui;* that's where I want to go—aboard
your *wagon-lit*, for Paris. *Voilà!*"—the girl
carefully gave the word three syllables—"*mon*
ticket *pour Paree!*" She opened her patent-
leather reticule, rummaged furiously therein,
brought out a handkerchief, a tiny mirror, a
packet of rice papers, and at last a folded and
punched ticket. This she displayed with a tri-
umphant flourish.

"*Voilà!* *Il dit* 'Miss Jane Gerson'; that's me
—*moi-meme*, I mean. And *il dit 'deux troncs';*
now you can't go behind that, can you? Where
is that other trunk?"

A whistle shrilled back beyond the swinging
doors of the station. Folk in the customs shed
began a hasty gathering together of parcels
and shawl straps, and a general exodus toward
the train sheds commenced. The girl on the
trunk looked appealingly about her; nothing
but bustle and confusion; no Samaritan to turn
aside and rescue a fair traveler fallen among
customs guards. Her eyes filled with trouble,
and for an instant her reliant mouth broke its

line of determination; the lower lip quivered suspiciously. Even the guard started to walk away.

"Oh, oh, please don't go!" Jane Gerson was on her feet, and her hands shot out in an impulsive appeal. "Oh, dear; maybe I forgot to tip you. Here, *attende au secours,* if you'll only find that other trunk before the train——"

"Pardon; but if I may be of any assistance——"

Miss Gerson turned. A tallish, old-young-looking man, in a gray lounge suit, stood heels together and bent stiffly in a bow. Nothing of the beau or the boulevardier about his face or manner. Miss Gerson accepted his intervention as heaven-sent.

"Oh, thank you ever so much! The guard, you see, doesn't understand good French. I just can't make him understand that one of my trunks is missing. And the train for Paris——"

Already the stranger was rattling incisive French at the guard. That official bowed low, and, with hands and lips, gave rapid explanation. The man in the gray lounge suit turned to the girl.

"A little misunderstanding, Miss—ah——"

"Gerson—Jane Gerson, of New York," she promptly supplied.

"A little misunderstanding, Miss Gerson. The customs guard says your other trunk has already been examined, passed, and placed on the baggage van. He was trying to tell you that it would be necessary for you to permit a porter to take this trunk to the train before time for starting. With your permission——"

The stranger turned and halloed to a porter, who came running. Miss Gerson had the trunk locked and strapped in no time, and it was on the shoulders of the porter.

"You have very little time, Miss Gerson. The train will be making a start directly. If I might—ah—pilot you through the station to the proper train shed. I am not presuming?"

"You are very kind," she answered hurriedly.

They set off, the providential Samaritan in the lead. Through the waiting-room and on to a broad platform, almost deserted, they went. A guard's whistle shrilled. The stranger tucked a helping hand under Jane Gerson's arm to steady her in the sharp sprint down a long aisle between tracks to where the Paris train stood. It began to move before they had reached its mid-length. A guard threw open a carriage door, in they hopped, and with a rattle of chains and banging of buffers the Express du Nord was off on its arrow flight from Calais to the capital.

The carriage, which was of the second class, was comfortably filled. Miss Gerson stumbled over the feet of a puffy Fleming nearest the door, was launched into the lap of a comfortably upholstered widow on the opposite seat, ricochetted back to jam an elbow into a French gentleman's spread newspaper, and finally was catapulted into a vacant space next to the window on the carriage's far side. She giggled, tucked the skirts of her pearl-gray duster about her, righted the chic sailor hat on her chestnut-brown head, and patted a stray wisp of hair back into place. Her meteor flight into and through the carriage disturbed her not a whit.

As for the Samaritan, he stood uncertainly in the narrow cross aisle, swaying to the swing of the carriage and reconnoitering seating possibilities. There was a place, a very

narrow one, next to the fat Fleming; also
there was a vacant place next to Jane Gerson.
The Samaritan caught the girl's glance in his
indecision, read in it something frankly com-
radely, and chose the seat beside her.

"Very good of you, I'm sure," he murmured.
"I did not wish to presume——"

"You're not," the girl assured, and there was
something so fresh, so ingenuous, in the tone
and the level glance of her brown eyes that
the Samaritan felt all at once distinctly satisfied with the cast of fortune that had thrown
him in the way of a distressed traveler. He
sat down with a lifting of the checkered Alpine
hat he wore and a stiff little bow from the
waist.

"If I may, Miss Gerson—I am Captain
Woodhouse, of the signal service."

"Oh!" The girl let slip a little gasp—the
meed of admiration the feminine heart always
pays to shoulder straps. "Signal service; that
means the army?"

"His majesty's service; yes, Miss Gerson."

"You are, of course, off duty?" she suggested, with the faintest possible tinge of regret

at the absence of the stripes and buttons that
spell "soldier" with the woman.

"You might say so, Miss Gerson.   Egypt—
the Nile country is my station.   I am on my
way back there after a bit of a vacation at
home—London I mean, of course."

She stole a quick side glance at the face of
her companion. A soldier's face it was, lean and
school-hardened and competent.   Lines about
the eyes and mouth—the stamp of the sun and
the imprint of the habit to command—had
taken from Captain Woodhouse's features
something of freshness and youth, though giving in return the index of inflexible will and
lust for achievement.   His smooth lips were
a bit thin, Jane Gerson thought, and the out-
shooting chin, almost squared at the angles,
marked Captain Woodhouse as anything but a
trifler or a flirt.   She was satisfied that nothing of presumption or forwardness on the part
of this hard-molded chap from Egypt would
give her cause to regret her unconventional
offer of friendship.

Captain Woodhouse, in his turn, had made
a satisfying, though covert, appraisal of his

---

traveling companion by means of a narrow
mirror inset above the baggage rack over the
opposite seat. Trim and petite of figure, which
was just a shade under the average for height
and plumpness; a small head set sturdily on a
round smooth neck; face the very embodiment
of independence and self-confidence, with its
brown eyes wide apart, its high brow under
the parting waves of golden chestnut, broad
humorous mouth, and tiny nose slightly nibbed
upward: Miss Up-to-the-Minute New York,
indeed! From the cocked red feather in her
hat to the dainty spatted boots Jane Gerson
appeared in Woodhouse's eyes a perfect, virile,
vividly alive American girl. He'd met her
kind before; had seen them browbeating ba-
zaar merchants in Cairo and riding desert
donkeys like strong young queens. The type
appealed to him.

The first stiffness of informal meeting wore
away speedily. The girl tactfully directed the
channel of conversation into lines familiar to
Woodhouse. What was Egypt like; who owned
the Pyramids, and why didn't the owners plant
a park around them and charge admittance?
Didn't he think Rameses and all those other

old Pharaohs had the right idea in advertising
—putting up stone billboards to last all time?
The questions came crisp and startling; Woodhouse found himself chuckling at the shrewd
incisiveness of them. Rameses an advertiser
and the Pyramids stone hoardings to carry all
those old boys' fame through the ages! He'd
never looked on them in that light before.

"I say, Miss Gerson, you'd make an excellent business person, now, really," the captain
voiced his admiration.

"Just cable that at my expense to old Pop
Hildebrand, of Hildebrand's department store,
New York," she flashed back at him. "I'm
trying to convince him of just that very
thing."

"Really, now; a department shop! What,
may I ask, do you have to do for—ah—Pop
Hildebrand?"

"Oh, I'm his foreign buyer," Jane answered,
with a conscious note of pride. "I'm over here
to buy gowns for the winter season, you see.
Paul Poiret—Worth—Paquin; you've heard of
those wonderful people, of course?"

"Can't say I have," the captain confessed,
with a rueful smile into the girl's brown eyes.

"Then you've never bought a Worth?" she challenged. "For if you had you'd not forget the name—or the price—very soon."

"Gowns—and things are not in my line, Miss Gerson," he answered simply, and the girl caught herself feeling a secret elation. A man who didn't know gowns couldn't be very intimately acquainted with women. And—well—

"And this Hildebrand, he sends you over here alone just to buy pretties for New York's wonderful women?" the captain was saying. "Aren't you just a bit—ah—nervous to be over in this part of the world—alone?"

"Not in the least," the girl caught him up. "Not about the alone part, I should say. Maybe I am fidgety and sort of worried about making good on the job. This is my first trip—my very first as a buyer for Hildebrand. And, of course, if I should fall down——"

"Fall down?" Woodhouse echoed, mystified. The girl laughed, and struck her left wrist a smart blow with her gloved right hand.

"There I go again—slang; 'vulgar American slang,' you'll call it. If I could only rattle off the French as easily as I do New Yorkese I'd be a wonder. I mean I'm afraid I won't make good."

"Oh!"

"But why should I worry about coming over alone?" Jane urged. "Lots of American girls come over here alone with an American flag pinned to their shirt-waists and wearing a Baedeker for a wrist watch. Nothing ever happens to them."

Captain Woodhouse looked out on the flying panorama of straw-thatched houses and fields heavy with green grain. He seemed to be balancing words. He glanced at the passenger across the aisle, a wizened little man, asleep. In a lowered voice he began:

"A woman alone—over here on the Continent at this time; why, I very much fear she will have great difficulties when the—ah—trouble comes."

"Trouble?" Jane's eyes were questioning.

"I do not wish to be an alarmist, Miss Gerson," Captain Woodhouse continued, hesitant. "Goodness knows we've had enough calamity shouters among the Unionists at home. But have you considered what you would do—how

you would get back to America in case of—
war?" The last word was almost a whisper.
"War?" she echoed. "Why, you don't mean
all this talk in the papers is——"

"Is serious, yes," Woodhouse answered quietly. "Very serious."

"Why, Captain Woodhouse, I thought you
had war talk every summer over here just as
our papers are filled each spring with gossip
about how Tesreau is going to jump to the
Feds, or the Yanks are going to be sold. It's
your regular midsummer outdoor sport over
here, this stirring up the animals."

Woodhouse smiled, though his gray eyes
were filled with something not mirth.

"I fear the animals are—stirred, as you say,
too far this time," he resumed. "The assassi-
nation of the Archduke Ferd——"

"Yes, I remember I did read something
about that in the papers at home. But arch-
dukes and kings have been killed before, and
no war came of it. In Mexico they murder a
president before he has a chance to send out
'At home' cards."

"Europe is so different from Mexico," her
companion continued, the lines of his face deep-

ening. "I am afraid you over in the States do not know the dangerous politics here; you are so far away; you should thank God for that. You are not in a land where one man —or two or three—may say, 'We will now go to war,' and then you go, willy-nilly."

The seriousness of the captain's speech and the fear that he could not keep from his eyes sobered the girl. She looked out on the sun-drenched plains of Pas de Calais, where toy villages, hedged fields, and squat farmhouses lay all in order, established, seeming for all time in the comfortable doze of security. The plodding manikins in the fields, the slumberous oxen drawing the harrows amid the beet rows, pigeons circling over the straw hutches by the tracks' side—all this denied the possibility of war's corrosion.

"Don't you think everybody is suffering from a bad dream when they say there's to be fighting?" she queried. "Surely it is impossible that folks over here would all consent to destroy this." She waved toward the peaceful countryside.

"A bad dream, yes. But one that will end in a nightmare," he answered. "Tell me, Miss

Gerson, when will you be through with your work in Paris, and on your way back to America?"

"Not for a month; that's sure. Maybe I'll be longer if I like the place."

Woodhouse pondered.

"A month. This is the tenth of July. I am afraid—— I say, Miss Gerson, please do not set me down for a meddler—this short acquaintance, and all that; but may I not urge on you that you finish your work in Paris and get back to England at least in two weeks?" The captain had turned, and was looking into the girl's eyes with an earnest intensity that startled her. "I can not tell you all I know, of course. I may not even know the truth, though I think I have a bit of it, right enough. But one of your sort—to be caught alone on this side of the water by the madness that is brewing! By George, I do not like to think of it!"

"I thank you, Captain Woodhouse, for your warning," Jane answered him, and impulsively she put out her hand to his. "But, you see, I'll have to run the risk. I couldn't go scampering back to New York like a scared pussy-cat just

because somebody starts a war over here. I'm
on trial. This is my first trip as buyer for
Hildebrand, and it's a case of make or break
with me. War or no war, I've got to make
good. Anyway"—this with a toss of her round
little chin—"I'm an American citizen, and nobody'll dare to start anything with me."

"Right you are!" Woodhouse beamed his
admiration. "Now we'll talk about those sky-
scrapers of yours. Everybody back from the
States has something to say about those famous
buildings, and I'm fairly burning for first-hand
information from one who knows them."

Laughingly she acquiesced, and the grim
shadow of war was pushed away from them,
though hardly forgotten by either. At the
man's prompting, Jane gave intimate pictures
of life in the New World metropolis, touching
with shrewd insight the fads and shams of
New York's denizens even as she exalted the
achievements of their restless energy.

Woodhouse found secret amusement and delight in her racy nervous speech, in the
dexterity of her idiom and patness of her
characterizations. Here was a new sort of
girl for him. Not the languid creature of

studied suppression and feeble enthusiasm he
had known, but a virile, vivid, sparkling
woman of a new land, whose impulses were as
unhindered as her speech was heterodox. She
was a woman who worked for her living; that
was a new type, too. Unafraid, she threw herself into the competition of a man's world; in-
sensibly she prided herself on her ability to
"make good"—expressive Americanism, that,—
under any handicap. She was a woman with
a "job"; Captain Woodhouse had never before
met one such.

Again, here was a woman who tried none
of the stale arts and tricks of coquetry; no
eyebrow strategy or maidenly simpering about
Jane Gerson. Once sure Woodhouse was what
she took him to be, a gentleman, the girl had
established a frank basis of comradeship that
took no reckoning of the age-old conventions
of sex allure and sex defense. The unconven-
tionality of their meeting weighed nothing
with her. Equally there was not a hint of
sophistication on the girl's part.

So the afternoon sped, and when the sun
dropped over the maze of spires and chimney
pots that was Paris, each felt regret at parting.

"To Egypt, yes," Woodhouse ruefully admitted. "A dreary deadly 'place in the sun' for me. To have met you, Miss Gerson; it has been delightful, quite."

"I hope," the girl said, as Woodhouse handed her into a taxi, "I hope that *if* that war comes it will find you still in Egypt, away from the firing-line."

"Not a fair thing to wish for a man in the service," Woodhouse answered, laughing. "I may be more happy when I say my best wish for you is that *when* the war comes it will find you a long way from Paris. Good-by, Miss Gerson, and good luck!"

Captain Woodhouse stood, heels together and hat in hand, while her taxi trundled off, a farewell flash of brown eyes rewarding him for the military correctness of his courtesy. Then he hurried to another station to take a train—not for a Mediterranean port and distant Egypt, but for Berlin.

CHAPTER II

FROM THE WILHELMSTRASSE

"IT would be wiser to talk in German," the woman said. "In these times French or English speech in Berlin——" she finished, with a lifting of her shapely bare shoulders, sufficiently eloquent. The waiter speeded his task of refilling the man's glass and discreetly withdrew.

"Oh, I'll talk in German quick enough," the man assented, draining his thin half bubble of glass down to the last fizzing residue in the stem. "Only just show me you've got the right to hear, and the good fat bank-notes to pay; that's all." He propped his sharp chin on a hand that shook slightly, and pushed his lean flushed face nearer hers. An owlish caution fought the wine fancies in his shifting lynx eyes under reddened lids; also there was admiration for the milk-white skin and ripe lips of the woman by his side. For an instant— half the time of a breath—a flash of loathing made the woman's eyes tigerish; but at once they changed again to mild bantering.

"So? Friend Billy Capper, of Brussels, has a touch of the spy fever himself, and distrusts an old pal?" She laughed softly, and one slim hand toyed with a heavy gold locket on her bosom. "Friend Billy Capper forgets old times and old faces—forgets even the matter of the Lord Fisher letters——"

"Chop it, Louisa!" The man called Capper lapsed into brusk English as he banged the stem of his wineglass on the damask. "No sense in raking that up again—just because I ask you a fair question—ask you to identify yourself in your new job."

"We go no further, Billy Capper," she returned, speaking swiftly in German; "not another word between us unless you obey my rule, and talk this language. Why did you get that message through to me to meet you here in the Café Riche to-night if you did not trust me? Why did you have me carry your offer to —to headquarters and come here ready to talk business if it was only to hum and haw about my identifying myself?"

The tenseness of exaggerated concentration

on Capper's gaunt face began slowly to dis-
solve. First the thin line of shaven lips flick-
ered and became weak at down-drawn corners;
then the frown faded from about the eyes, and
the beginnings of tears gathered there.
Shrewdness and the stamp of cunning sped
entirely, and naught but weakness remained.

"Louisa—Louisa, old pal; don't be hard on
poor Billy Capper," he mumbled. "I'm down,
girl—away down again. Since they kicked me
out at Brussels I haven't had a shilling to bless
myself with. Can't go back to England—you
know that; the French won't have me, and here
I am, my dinner clothes my only stock in trade
left, and you even having to buy the wine." A
tear of self-pity slipped down the hard drain
of his cheek and splashed on his hand. "But
I'll show 'em, Louisa! They can't kick me out
of the Brussels shop like a dog and not pay for
it! I know too much, I do!"

"And what you know about the Brussels
shop you want to sell to the—Wilhelmstrasse?"
the woman asked tensely.

"Yes, if the Wilhelmstrasse is willing to pay
well for it," Capper answered, his lost cunning
returning in a bound.

"I am authorized to judge how much your information is worth," his companion declared, leveling a cold glance into Capper's eyes. "You can tell me what you know, and depend on me to pay well, or—we part at once."

"But, Louisa"—again the whine—"how do I know you're what you say? You've flown high since you and I worked together in the Brussels shop. The Wilhelmstrasse—most perfect spy machine in the world! How I'd like to be in your shoes, Louisa!"

She detached the heavy gold locket from the chain on her bosom, with a quick twist of slim fingers had one side of the case open, then laid the locket before him, pointing to a place on the bevel of the case. Capper swept up the trinket, looked searchingly for an instant at the spot the woman had designated, and returned the locket to her hand.

"Your number in the Wilhelmstrasse," he whispered in awe. "Genuine, no doubt. Saw the same sort of mark once before in Rome. All right. Now, listen, Louisa. What I'm going to tell you about where Brussells stands in this—this business that's brewing will make the German general staff sit up." The woman

inclined her head toward Capper's. He, looking not at her but out over the rich plain of
brocades, broadcloths and gleaming shoulders,
began in a monotone:

"When the war comes—the day the war
starts, French artillerymen will be behind the
guns at Namur. The English——"

The Hungarian orchestra of forty strings
swept into a wild gipsy chant. Dissonances,
fierce and barbaric, swept like angry tides over
the brilliant floor of the café. Still Capper
talked on, and the woman called Louisa bent
her jewel-starred head to listen. Her face, the
face of a fine animal, was set in rapt attention.

"You mark my words," he finished, "when
the German army enters Brussels proof of
what I'm telling you will be there. Yes, in a
pigeonhole of the foreign-office safe those joint
plans between England and Belgium for resist-
ing invasion from the eastern frontier. If the
Germans strike as swiftly as I think they will
the foreign-office Johnnies will be so flustered
in moving out they'll forget these papers I'm
telling you about. Then your Wilhelmstrasse
will know they've paid for the truth when they
paid Billy Capper."

Capper eagerly reached for his glass, and, finding it empty, signaled the waiter.

"I'll buy this one, Louisa," he said grandiloquently. "Can't have a lady buying *me* wine all night." He gave the order. "You're going to slip me some bank-notes to-night—right now, aren't you, Louisa, old pal?" Capper anxiously honed his cheeks with a hand that trembled. The woman's eyes were narrowed in thought.

"If I give you anything to-night, Billy Capper, you'll get drunker than you are now, and how do I know you won't run to the first English secret-service man you meet and blab?"

"Louisa! Louisa! Don't say that!" Great fear and great yearning sat in Capper's filmed eyes. "You know I'm honest, Louisa! You wouldn't milk me this way—take all the info I've got and then throw me over like a dog!" Cold scorn was in her glance.

"Maybe I might manage to get you a position —with the Wilhelmstrasse." She named the great secret-service office under her breath. "You can't go back to England, to be sure; but you might be useful in the Balkans, where you're not known, or even in Egypt. You have your good points, Capper; you're a sly little weasel—when you're sober. Perhaps——"

"Yes, yes; get me a job with the Wilhelm-strasse, Louisa!" Capper was babbling in an agony of eagerness. "You know my work. You can vouch for me, and you needn't mention that business of the Lord Fisher letters; you were tarred pretty much with the same brush there, Louisa. But, come, be a good sport; pay me at least half of what you think my info's worth, and I'll take the rest out in salary checks, if you get me that job. I'm broke, Louisa!" His voice cracked in a sob. "Absolutely stony broke!"

She sat toying with the stem of her wine-glass while Capper's clasped hands on the table opened and shut themselves without his volition. Finally she made a swift move of one hand to her bodice, withdrew it with a bundle of notes crinkling between the fingers.

"Three hundred marks now, Billy Capper," she said. The man echoed the words lovingly. "Three hundred now, and my promise to try to get a number for you with—my people. That's fair?"

"Fair as can be, Louisa." He stretched out

clawlike fingers to receive the thin sheaf of notes she counted from her roll. "Here comes the wine—the wine I'm buying. We'll drink to my success at landing a job with—your people."

"For me no more to-night," the woman answered. "My cape, please." She rose.

"But, I say!" Capper protested. "Just one more bottle—the bottle I'm buying. See, here it is all proper and cooled. Marks the end of my bad luck, so it does. You won't refuse to drink with me to my good luck that's coming?"

"Your good luck is likely to stop short with that bottle, Billy Capper," she said, her lips parting in a smile half scornful. "You know how wine has played you before. Better stop now while luck's with you."

"Hanged if I do!" he answered stubbornly. "After these months of hand to mouth and begging for a nasty pint of ale in a common pub—leave good wine when it's right under my nose? Not me!" Still protesting against her refusal to drink with him the wine he would pay for himself—the man made that a point of injured honor—Capper grudgingly helped place the cape of web lace over his companion's white shoulders, and accompanied her to her taxi.

"If you're here this time to-morrow night—and sober," were her farewell words, "I may bring you your number in the—you understand; that and your commission to duty."

"God bless you, Louisa, girl!" Capper stammered thickly. "I'll not fail you."

He watched the taxi trundle down the brilliant mirror of Unter den Linden, a sardonic smile twisting his lips. Then he turned back to the world of light and perfume and wine—the world from which he had been barred these many months and for which the starved body of him had cried out in agony. His glass stood brimming; money crinkled in his pocket; there were eyes for him and fair white shoulders. Billy Capper, discredited spy, had come to his own once more.

The orchestra was booming a rag-time, and the chorus on the stage of the Winter Garden came plunging to the footlights, all in line, their black legs kicking out from the skirts like thrusting spindles in some marvelous engine of stagecraft. They screeched the final line of a Germanized coon song, the cymbals clanged "Zam-m-m!" and folk about the clustered tables pattered applause. Captain Woodhouse, at a table by himself, pulled a wafer of a watch from his waistcoat pocket, glanced at its face and looked back at the rococo entrance arches, through which the late-comers were streaming.

"Henry Sherman, do you think Kitty ought to see this sort of thing? It's positively indecent!"

The high-pitched nasal complaint came from a table a little to the right of the one where Woodhouse was sitting.

"There, there, mother! Now, don't go taking all the joy outa life just because you're seeing something that would make the minister back in Kewanee roll his eyes in horror. This is Germany, mother!"

Out of the tail of his eye, Woodhouse could see the family group wherein Mrs. Grundy had sat down to make a fourth. A blocky little man with a red face and a pinky-bald head, whose clothes looked as if they had been whip-sawed out of the bolt; a comfortably stout matron wearing a bonnet which even to the

untutored masculine eye betrayed its pro-
vincialism; a slim slip of a girl of about nineteen with a face like a choir boy's—these were
the American tourists whose voices had at-
tracted Woodhouse's attention. He played an
amused eavesdropper, all the more interested
because they were Americans, and since a certain day on the Calais-Paris express, a week
or so gone, he'd had reason to be interested in
all Americans.

"I'm surprised at you, Henry, defending
such an exhibition as this," the matron's high
complaint went on, "when you were mighty
shocked at the bare feet of those innocent
Greek dancers the Ladies' Aid brought to give
an exhibition on Mrs. Peck's lawn."

"Well, mother, that was different," the genial little chap answered. "Kewanee's a good
little town, and should stay proper. Berlin,
from what I can see, is a pretty bad big town
—and don't care." He pulled a heavy watch
from his waistcoat pocket and consulted it.
"Land's sakes, mother; seven o'clock back
home, and the bell's just ringing for Wednes-
day-night prayer meeting! Maybe since it's
prayer-meeting night we might be passing our

time better than by looking at this—ah—exhibition."

There was a scraping of chairs, then:

"Henry, I tell you he does look like Albert Downs—the living image!" This from the woman, sotto voce.

"Sh! mother! What would Albert Downs be doing in Berlin?" The daughter was reproving.

"Well, Kitty, they say curiosity once killed a cat; but I'm going to have a better look. I'd swear——"

Woodhouse was slightly startled when he saw the woman from America utilize the clumsy subterfuge of a dropped handkerchief to step into a position whence she could look at his face squarely. Also he was annoyed. He did not care to be stared at under any circumstances, particularly at this time. The alert and curious lady saw his flush of annoyance, flushed herself, and joined her husband and daughter.

"Well, if I didn't know Albert Downs had a livery business which he couldn't well leave," floated back the hoarse whisper, "I'd say that was him setting right there in that chair."

"Come, mother, bedtime and after—in Berlin," was the old gentleman's admonition. Woodhouse heard their retreating footsteps, and laughed in spite of his temporary chagrin at the American woman's curiosity. He was just reaching for his watch a second time when a quick step sounded on the gravel behind him. He turned. A woman of ripe beauty had her hand outstretched in welcome. She was the one Billy Capper had called Louisa. Captain Woodhouse rose and grasped her hand warmly.

"Ah! So good of you! I've been expecting——"

"Yes, I'm late. I could not come earlier." Salutation and answer were in German, fluently spoken on the part of each.

"You will not be followed?" Woodhouse asked, assisting her to sit. She laughed shortly.

"Hardly, when a bottle of champagne is my rival. The man will be well entertained—too well."

"I have been thinking," Woodhouse continued gravely, "that a place hardly as public as this would have been better for our meeting. Perhaps——"

"You fear the English agents? Pah! They have ears for keyholes only; they do not expect to use them in a place where there is light and plenty of people. You know their clumsiness." Woodhouse nodded. His eyes traveled slowly over the bold beauty of the woman's face.

"The man Capper will do for the stalking horse—a willing nag," went on the woman in a half whisper across the table. "You know the ways of the Wilhelmstrasse. Capper is what we call 'the target.' The English suspect him. They will catch him; you get his number and do the work in safety. We have one man to draw their fire, another to accomplish the deed. We'll let the English bag him at Malta —a word placed in the right direction will fix that—and you'll go on to Alexandria to do the real work."

"Good, good!" Woodhouse agreed.

"The Wilhelmstrasse will give him a number, and send him on this mission on my recommendation; I had that assurance before ever I met the fellow to-night. They—the big people —know little Capper's reputation, and, as a matter of fact, I think they are convinced he's a little less dangerous working for the Wilhelm-

strasse than against it. At Malta the arrest
—the firing squad at dawn—and the English
are convinced they've nipped something big in
the bud, whereas they've only put out of the
way a dangerous little weasel who's ready to
bite any hand that feeds him."

Woodhouse's level glance never left the eyes
of the woman called Louisa; it was alert, appraising.

"But if there should be some slip-up at
Malta," he interjected. "If somehow this Capper should get through to Alexandria, wouldn't
that make it somewhat embarrassing for me?"

"Not at all, my dear Woodhouse," she caught
him up, with a little pat on his hand. "His instructions will be only to report to So-and-so
at Alexandria; he will not have the slightest
notion what work he is to do there. You can
slip in unsuspected by the English, and the
trick will be turned."

For a minute Woodhouse sat watching the
cavortings of a dancer on the stage. Finally
he put a question judiciously:

"The whole scheme, then, is——"

"This," she answered quickly. "Captain
Woodhouse—the real Woodhouse, you know—

is to be transferred from his present post at Wady Halfa, on the Nile, to Gibraltar—transfer is to be announced in the regular way within a week. As a member of the signal service he will have access to the signal tower on the Rock when he takes his new post, and that, as you know, will be very important."

"Very important!" Woodhouse echoed dryly.

"This Woodhouse arrives in Alexandria to await the steamer from Suez to Gib. He has no friends there—that much we know. Three men of the Wilhelmstrasse are waiting there, whose business it is to see that the real Woodhouse does not take the boat for Gib. They expect a man from Berlin to come to them, bearing a number from the Wilhelmstrasse— the man who is to impersonate Woodhouse and as such take his place in the garrison on the Rock. There are two others of the Wilhelmstrasse at Gibraltar already; they, too, are eagerly awaiting the arrival of 'Woodhouse' from Alexandria. Capper, with a number, will start from Berlin for Alexandria. Capper will never arrive in Alexandria. You will."

"With a number—*the* number expected?" the man asked.

"If you are clever en route—yes," she answered, with a smile. "Wine, remember, is Billy Capper's best friend—and worst enemy."

"Then I will hear from you as to the time and route of departure for Alexandria?"

"To the very hour, yes. And, now, dear friend——"

Interruption came suddenly from the stage. The manager, in shirt-sleeves and with hair wildly rumpled over his eyes, came prancing out from the wings. He held up a pudgy hand to check the orchestra. Hundreds about the tables rose in a gust of excitement, of questioning wonder.

"*Herren!*" The stage manager's bellow carried to the farthest arches of the Winter Garden. "News just published by the general staff: Russia has mobilized five divisions on the frontier of East Prussia and Galicia!"

Not a sound save the sharp catching of breath over all the acre of tables. Then the stage manager nodded to the orchestra leader, and in a fury the brass mouths began to bray. Men climbed on table tops, women stood on chairs, and all—all sang in tremendous chorus:

"*Deutschland, Deutschland üeber alles!*"

CHAPTER III

BILLY CAPPER AT PLAY

THE night of July twenty-sixth. The scene is the table-cluttered sidewalk before the Café Pytheas, where the Cours St. Louis flings its night tide of idlers into the broader stream of the Cannebière, Marseilles' Broadway—the white street of the great Provençal port. Here at the crossing of these two streets summer nights are incidents to stick in the traveler's mind long after he sees the gray walls of the Château d'If fade below the steamer's rail. The flower girls in their little pulpits pressing dewy violets and fragrant clusters of rosebuds upon the strollers with persuasive eloquence; the mystical eyes of hooded Moors who see everything as they pass, yet seem to see so little; jostling Greeks, Levantines, burnoosed Jews from Algiers and red-trousered Senegalese—all the color from the hot lands of the Mediterranean is there.

But on the night of July twenty-sixth the old

spirit of indolence, of pleasure seeking, flirtation, intriguing, which was wont to make this heart of arc-light life in Marseilles pulse languorously, was gone. Instead, an electric tenseness was abroad, pervading, infectious. About each sidewalk table heads were clustered close in conference, and eloquent hands aided explosive argument. Around the news kiosk at the Café Pytheas corner a constant stream eddied. Men snatched papers from the pile, spread them before their faces, and blundered into their fellow pedestrians as they walked, buried in the inky columns. Now and again half-naked urchins came charging down the Cannebière, waving shinplaster extras above their heads—"*L'Allemagne s'arme! La guerre vient!*" Up from the Quai marched a dozen sailors from a torpedo boat, arms linked so that they almost spanned the Cannebière. Their red-tasseled caps were pushed back at cocky angles on their black heads, and as they marched they shouted in time: "*A Berlin! Hou—hou!*"

The black shadow of war—the first hallucinations of the great madness—gripped Marseilles.

For Captain Woodhouse, just in from Berlin
that evening, all this swirling excitement had
but an incidental interest. He sat alone by
one of the little iron tables before the Café
Pytheas, sipping his *boc*, and from time to time
his eyes carelessly followed the eddying of the
swarm about the news kiosk. Always his attention would come back, however, to center on
the thin shoulders of a man sitting fifteen or
twenty feet away with a wine cooler by his
side. He could not see the face of the wine
drinker; he did not want to. All he cared to
do was to keep those thin shoulders always in
sight. Each time the solicitous waiter renewed
the bottle in the wine cooler Captain Woodhouse nodded grimly, as a doctor might when
he recognized the symptoms of advancing fever
in a patient.

So for two days, from Berlin across to Paris,
and now on this third day here in the Mediterranean port, Woodhouse had kept ever in sight
those thin shoulders and that trembling hand
beyond the constantly crooking elbow. Not a
pleasant task; he had come to loathe and abom-
inate the very wrinkles in the back of that
shiny coat. But a very necessary duty it was

for Captain Woodhouse to shadow Mr. Billy
Capper until—the right moment should arrive.
They had come down on the same express together from Paris. Woodhouse had observed
Capper when he checked his baggage, a single
shoddy hand-bag, for *La Vendée*, the French
line ship sailing with the dawn next morning
for Alexandria and Port Said via Malta. Capper had squared his account at the Hotel Allées
de Meilhan, for the most part a bill for absinth
frappés, after dinner that night, and was now
enjoying the night life of Marseilles in antici-
pation, evidently, of carrying direct to the
steamer with him as his farewell from France
all of the bottled laughter of her peasant girls
he could accommodate.

The harsh memories of how he had been
forced to drink the bitter lees of poverty during the lean months rode Billy Capper hard,
and this night he wanted to fill all the starved
chambers of his soul with the robust music of
the grape. So he drank with a purpose and
purposefully. That he drank alone was a matter of choice with Capper; he could have had
a pair of dark eyes to glint over a goblet into
his had he wished—indeed, opportunities al-

most amounted to embarrassment. But to all advances from the fair, Billy Capper returned merely an impolite leer. He knew from beforetime that he was his one best companion when the wine began to warm him. So he squared himself to his pleasure with an abandoned rakishness expressed in the set of his thin shoulders and the forward droop of his head.

Woodhouse, who watched, noted only one peculiarity in Capper's conduct: The drinker nursed his stick, a plain, crook-handled malacca, with a tenderness almost maternal. It never left his hands. Once when Capper dropped it and the waiter made to prop the stick against a near-by chair, the little spy leaped to his feet and snatched the cane away with a growl. Thereafter he propped his chin on the handle, only removing this guard when he had to tip his head back for another draft of champagne.

Eleven o'clock came. Capper rose from the table and looked owlishly about him. Woodhouse quickly turned his back to the man, and was absorbed in the passing strollers. When he looked back again Capper was slowly and a

little unsteadily making his way around the
corner into the Cannebière. Woodhouse followed, sauntering. Capper began a dilatory
exploration of the various cafés along the white
street; his general course was toward the city's
slums about the Quai. Woodhouse, dawdling
about tree boxes and dodging into shadows by
black doorways, found his quarry easy to trail.
And he knew that each of Capper's sojourns in
an oasis put a period to the length of the pur-
suit. The time for him to act drew appreciably
nearer with every tipping of that restless
elbow.

Midnight found them down in the reek and
welter of the dives and sailors' frolic grounds.
Now the trailer found his task more difficult,
inasmuch as not only his quarry but he himself was marked by the wolves. Dances in
smoke-wreathed rooms slackened when Capper
lurched in, found a seat and ordered a drink.
Women with cheeks carmined like poppies
wanted to make predatory love to him; dock
rats drew aside and consulted in whispers.
When Capper retreated from an evil dive on
the very edge of the Quai, Woodhouse, waiting
by the doors, saw that he was not the only

shadower. Close against the dead walls flank-
ing the narrow pavement a slinking figure
twisted and writhed after the drunkard, now
spread-eagling all over the street.

Woodhouse quickened his pace on the opposite sidewalk. The street was one lined with
warehouses, their closely shuttered windows
the only eyes. Capper dropped his stick, labor-
iously halted, and started to go back for it.
That instant the shadow against the walls detached itself and darted for the victim. Woodhouse leaped to the cobbles and gained Capper's
side just as he dropped like a sack of rags
under a blow from the dock rat's fist.

"Son of a pig! This is my meat; you clear
out!" The humped black beetle of a man
straddling the sprawling Capper whipped a
knife from his girdle and faced Woodhouse.
Quicker than light the captain's right arm shot
out; a thud as of a maul on an empty wine butt,
and the Apache turned a half somersault,
striking the cobbles with the back of his head.
Woodhouse stooped, lifted the limp Capper
from the street stones, and staggered with him
to the lighted avenue of the Cannebière, a block
away. He hailed a late-cruising fiacre, propped

Capper in the seat, and took his place beside him.

"To *La Vendée,* Quai de la Fraternité!" Woodhouse ordered.

The driver, wise in the ways of the city, asked no questions, but clucked to his crow bait. Woodhouse turned to make a quick examination of the unconscious man by his side. He feared a stab wound; he found nothing but a nasty cut on the head, made by brass knuckles. With the wine helping, any sort of a blow would have put Capper out, he reflected.

Woodhouse turned his back on the bundle of clothes and reached for the malacca stick. Even in his coma its owner grasped it tenaciously at midlength. Without trying to disengage the clasp, Woodhouse gripped the wood near the crook of the handle with his left hand while with his right he applied torsion above. The crook turned on hidden threads and came off in his hand. An exploring forefinger in the exposed hollow end of the cane encountered a rolled wisp of paper. Woodhouse pocketed this, substituted in its place a thin clean sheet torn from a card-case memorandum, then screwed the crook on the stick down on the secret receptacle. By the light of a match he assured himself the paper he had taken from the cane was what he wanted.

"Larceny from the person—guilty," he murmured, with a wry smile of distaste. "But assault—unpremeditated."

The conveyance trundled down a long spit of stone and stopped by the side of a black hull, spotted with round eyes of light. The driver, scenting a tip, helped Woodhouse lift Capper to the ground and prop him against a bulkhead. A bos'n, summoned from *La Vendée* by the cabby's shrill whistle, heard Woodhouse's explanation with sympathy.

"Occasionally, yes, m'sieu, the passengers from Marseilles have these regrets at parting," he gravely commented, accepting the ticket Woodhouse had rummaged from the unconscious man's wallet and a crinkled note from Woodhouse's. Up the gangplank, feet first, went the new agent of the Wilhelmstrasse. The one who called himself "captain in his majesty's signal service" returned to his hotel.

At dawn, *La Vendée* cleared the harbor for Alexandria via Malta, bearing a very sick Billy Capper to his destiny. Five hours later the

Castle liner, *Castle Claire*, for the Cape via Alexandria and Suez direct, sailed out of the Old Port, among her passengers a Captain Woodhouse.

CHAPTER IV,

MANY a long starlit hour alone on the deck of the *Castle Claire* Captain Woodhouse found himself tortured by a persistent vision. Far back over the northern horizon lay Europe, trembling and breathless before the imminent disaster—a great field of grain, each stalk bearing for its head the helmeted head of a man. Out of the east came a glow, which spread from boundary to boundary, waxed stronger in the wind of hate. Finally the fire, devastating, insensate, began its sweep through the close-standing mazes of the grain. Somewhere in this fire-glow and swift leveling under the scythe of the flame was a girl, alone, appalled. Woodhouse could see her as plainly as though a cinema was unreeling swift pictures before him—the girl caught in this vast acreage of fire, in the standing grain, with destruction drawing nearer in

incredible strides. He saw her wide eyes, her
streaming hair—saw her running through the
grain, whose heads were the helmeted heads of
men. Her hands groped blindly and she was
calling—calling, with none to come in aid.
Jane Gerson alone in the face of Europe's
burning!

Strive as he would, Woodhouse could not
screen this picture from his eyes. He tried to
hope that ere this, discretion had conquered her
resolution to "make good," and that she had
fled from Paris, one of the great army of
refugees who had already begun to pour out
of the gates of France when he passed through
the war-stunned capital a few days before.
But, no; there was no mistaking the determination he had read in those brown eyes that day
on the express from Calais. "I couldn't go
scampering back to New York just because
somebody starts a war over here." Brave, yes;
but hers was the bravery of ignorance. This
little person from the States, on her first venture into the complex life of the Continent,
could not know what war there would mean;
the terror and magnitude of it. And now
where was she? In Paris, caught in its

hysteria of patriotism and darkling fear of
what the morrow would bring forth? Or had
she started for England, and become wedged
in the jam of terrified thousands battling for
place on the Channel steamers? Was her fine
self-reliance upholding her, or had the crisis
sapped her courage and thrown her back on
the common helplessness of women before disaster?

Captain Woodhouse, the self-sufficient and
aloof, whose training had been all toward suppression of every instinct save that in the line
of duty, was surprised at himself. That a
little American *inconnu*—a "business person,"
he would have styled her under conditions less
personal—should have come into his life in this
definite way was, to say the least, highly
irregular. The man tried to swing his reason
as a club against his heart—and failed miser-
ably. No, the fine brave spirit that looked out
of those big brown eyes would not be argued
out of court. Jane Gerson was a girl who was
different, and that very difference was altogether alluring. Woodhouse caught himself
going over the incidents of their meeting.
Fondly he reviewed scraps of their conversa-

tion on the train, lingering on the pat slang
she used so unconsciously.

Was it possible Jane Gerson ever had a
thought for Captain Woodhouse? The man
winced a little at this speculation. Had it been
fair of him when he so glibly practised a deception on her? If she knew what his present
business was, would she understand; would she
approve? Could this little American ever
know, or believe, that some sorts of service
were honorable?

Just before the *Castle Claire* raised the
breakwater of Alexandria came a wireless,
which was posted at the head of the saloon
companionway:

"Germany declares war on Russia. German
flying column reported moving through Luxem-
burg on Belgium."

The fire was set to the grain.

Upon landing, Captain Woodhouse's first
business was to go to a hotel on the Grand
Square, which is the favorite stopping place of
officers coming down from the Nile country.
He fought his way through the predatory

hordes of yelling donkey boys and obsequious dragomans at the door, and entered the palm-shaded court, which served as office and lounge. Woodhouse paused for a second behind a screen of palm leaves and cast a quick eye around the court. None of the loungers there was known to him. He strode to the desk.

"Ah, sir, a room with bath, overlooking the gardens on the north side—very cool." The Greek clerk behind the desk smiled a welcome.

"Perhaps," Woodhouse answered shortly, and he turned the register around to read the names of the recent comers. On the first page he found nothing to interest him; but among the arrivals of the day before he saw this entry: "C. G. Woodhouse, Capt. Sig. Service; Wady Halfa." After it was entered the room number: "210."

Woodhouse read right over the name and turned another page a bit impatiently. This he scanned with seeming eagerness, while the clerk stood with pen poised.

"Um! When is the first boat out for Gibraltar?" Woodhouse asked.

"Well, sir, the *Princess Mary* is due to sail at dawn day after to-morrow," the Greek answered judiciously. "She is reported at Port Said to-day, but, of course, the war——"

Woodhouse turned away.

"But you wish a room, sir—nice room, with bath, overlooking——"

"No."

"You expected to find a friend, then?"

"Not here," Woodhouse returned bruskly, and passed out into the blinding square.

He strode swiftly around the statue of Mehemet Ali and plunged into the bedlam crowd filling a side street. With sure sense of direction, he threaded the narrow alleyways and by-streets until he had come to the higher part of the mongrel city, near the Rosetta Gate. There he turned into a little French hotel, situated far from the disordered pulse of the city's heart; a sort of pension, it was, known only to the occasional discriminating tourist. Maitre Mouquère was proud of the anonymity his house preserved, and abhorred poor, driven Cook's slaves as he would a plague. In his Cap de Liberté one was lost to all the world of Alexandria.

Thither the captain's baggage had been sent direct from the steamer. After a glass with

Maitre Mouquère and a half hour's discussion of the day's great news, Woodhouse pleaded a touch of the sun, and went to his room. There he remained, until the gold of sunset had faded from the Mosque of Omar's great dome and all the city from Pharos and its harbor hedge of masts to El Meks winked with lights. Then he took carriage to the railroad station and entrained for Ramleh. What South Kensington is to London and the Oranges are to New York, Ramleh is to Alexandria—the suburb of homes. There pretty villas lie in the lap of the delta's greenery, skirted by canals, cooled by the winds off Aboukir Bay and shaded by great palms—the one beauty spot in all the hybrid product of East and West that is the present city of Alexander.

Remembering directions he had received in Berlin, Woodhouse threaded shaded streets until he paused before a stone gateway set in a high wall. On one of the pillars a small brass plate was inset. By the light of a near-by arc, Woodhouse read the inscription on it:

EMIL KOCH, M. D.,
32 Queen's Terrace.

He threw back his shoulders with a sudden
gesture, which might have been taken for that
of a man about to make a plunge, and rang
the bell. The heavy wooden gate, filling all the
space of the arch, was opened by a tall Numidian in house livery of white. He nodded an
affirmative to Woodhouse's question, and led the
way through an avenue of flaming hibiscus to
a house, set far back under heavy shadow of
acacias. On every hand were gardens, rank
foliage shutting off this walled yard from the
street and neighboring dwellings. The heavy
gate closed behind the visitor with a sharp
snap. One might have said that Doctor Koch
lived in pretty secure isolation.

Woodhouse was shown into a small room off
the main hall, by its furnishings and position
evidently a waiting-room for the doctor's pa-
tients. The Numidian bowed, and disappeared.
Alone, Woodhouse rose and strolled aimlessly
about the room, flipped the covers of magazines on the table, picked up and hefted the
bronze Buddha on the onyx mantel, noted, with
a careless glance, the position of the two windows in relation to the entrance door and the

folding doors, now shut, which doubtless gave
on the consultation room. As he was regarding these doors they rolled back and a short
thickset man, with a heavy mane of iron-gray
hair and black brush of beard, stood between
them. He looked at Woodhouse through thick-
lensed glasses, which gave to his stare a curiously intent bent.

"My office hours are from two to four, after-
noons," Doctor Koch said. He spoke in English, but his speech was burred by a slight
heaviness on the aspirants, reminiscent of his
mother tongue. The doctor did not ask Woodhouse to enter the consultation room, but continued standing between the folding doors,
staring fixedly through his thick lenses.

"I know that, Doctor," Woodhouse began
apologetically, following the physician's lead
and turning his tongue to English. "But, you
see, in a case like mine I have to intrude"—it
was "haf" and "indrude" as Woodhouse gave
these words—"because I could not be here during your office hours. You will pardon?"

Doctor Koch's eyes widened just perceptibly
at the hint of a Germanic strain in his visitor's

speech—just a hint quickly glossed over. But still he remained standing in his former attitude of annoyance.

"Was the sun, then, too hot to bermit you to come to my house during regular office hours? At nights I see no batients—bositively none."

"The sun—perhaps," Woodhouse replied guardedly. "But as I happened just to arrive to-day from Marseilles, and your name was strongly recommended to me as one to consult in a case such as mine——"

"Where was my name recommended to you, and by whom?" Doctor Koch interrupted in sudden interest.

Woodhouse looked at him steadily. "In Berlin—and by a friend of yours," he answered.

"Indeed?" The doctor stepped back from the doors, and motioned his visitor into the consultation room.

Woodhouse stepped into a large room lighted by a single green-shaded reading lamp, which threw a white circle of light straight down upon a litter of thin-bladed scalpels in a glass dish of disinfectant on a table. The shadowy outlines of an operating chair, of high-shouldered bookcases, and the dull glint of instruments in a long glass case were almost imperceptible because of the centering of all light upon the glass dish of knives. Doctor Koch dragged a chair out from the shadows, and, carelessly enough, placed it in the area of radiance; he motioned Woodhouse to sit. The physician leaned carelessly against an arm of the operating chair; his face was in the shadow save where reflected light shone from his glasses, giving them the aspect of detached eyes.

"So, a friend—a friend in Berlin told you to consult me, eh? Berlin is a long way from Ramleh—especially in these times. Greater physicians than I live in Berlin. Why——"

"My friend in Berlin told me you were the only physician who could help me in my peculiar trouble." Imperceptibly the accenting of the aspirants in Woodhouse's speech grew more marked; his voice took on a throaty character. "By some specialists my life even has been set to end in a certain year, so sure is fate for those afflicted like myself."

"So? What year is it, then, you die?" Doctor Koch's strangely detached eyes—those

eyes of glass glowing dimly in the shadow—
seemed to flicker palely with a light all their
own. Captain Woodhouse, sitting under the
white spray of the shaded incandescent, looked
up carelessly to meet the stare.

"Why, they give me plenty of time to enjoy
myself," he answered, with a light laugh. "They
say in 1932——"

"Nineteen thirty-two!" Doctor Koch stepped
lightly to the closed folding doors, trundled
them back an inch to assure himself nobody
was in the waiting-room, then closed and
locked them. He did similarly by a hidden door
on the opposite side of the room, which Woodhouse had not seen. After that he pulled a
chair close to his visitor and sat down, his
knees almost touching the other's. He spoke
very low, in German:

"If your trouble is so serious that you will
die—in 1932, I must, of course, examine you
for—symptoms."

For half a minute the two men looked fixedly
at each other. Woodhouse's right hand went
slowly to the big green scarab stuck in his
cravat. He pulled the pin out, turned it over

in his fingers, and by pressure caused the
scarab to pop out of the gold-backed setting
holding it. The bit of green stone lay in the
palm of his left hand, its back exposed. In the
hollowed back of the beetle was a small square
of paper, folded minutely. This Woodhouse
removed, unfolded and passed to the physician.
The latter seized it avidly, holding it close to
his spectacled eyes, and then spreading it
against the light as if to read a secret water
mark. A smile struggled through the jungle
of his beard. He found Woodhouse's hand and
grasped it warmly.

"Your symptom tallies with my diagnosis,
Nineteen Thirty-two," he began rapidly. "Five
days ago we heard from—the Wilhelmstrasse
—you would come. We have expected you each
day, now. Already we have got word through
to our friends at Gibraltar of the plan; they
are waiting for you."

"Good!" Woodhouse commented. He was
busy refolding the thin slip of paper that had
been his talisman, and fitting it into the back
of the scarab. "Woodhouse—he is already at
the Hotel Khedive; saw his name on the regis-

ter when I landed from the *Castle* this morning." Now the captain was talking in familiar
German.

"Quite so," Doctor Koch put in. "Woodhouse came down from Wady Halfa yesterday. Our man up there had advised of the
time of his arrival in Alexandria to the
minute. The captain has his ticket for
the *Princess Mary,* which sails for Gibraltar
day after to-morrow at dawn."

Number Nineteen Thirty-two listened to
Doctor Koch's outlining of the plot with set
features; only his eyes showed that he was
acutely alive to every detail. Said he:

"But Woodhouse—this British captain who's
being transferred from the Nile country to the
Rock; has he ever served there before? If he
has, why, when I get there—when I am Captain Woodhouse, of the signal service—I will
be embarrassed if I do not know the ropes."

"Seven years ago Woodhouse was there for a
very short time," Doctor Koch explained. "New
governor since then—changes all around in
the personnel of the staff, I don't doubt. You'll
have no trouble."

Silence between them for a minute, broken by the captain:

"Our friends at Gib—who are they, and how will I know them?"

The doctor bent a sudden glance of suspicion upon the lean face before him. His thick lips clapped together stubbornly.

"Aha, my dear friend; you are asking questions. In my time at Berlin the Wilhelmstrasse taught that all orders and information came from above—and from there only. Why——"

"I suppose in default of other information I may ask the governor to point out the Wilhelmstrasse men," Woodhouse answered, with a shrug. "I was told at Berlin I would learn all that was necessary to me as I went along, therefore, I supposed——"

"Come—come!" Doctor Koch patted the other's shoulder, with a heavy joviality. "So you will. When you arrive at Gib, put up at the Hotel Splendide, and you will not be long learning who your friends are. I, for instance, did not hesitate overmuch to recognize you, and I am under the eyes of the English here at every turn, even though I am a naturalized English citizen—and of undoubted loyalty." He finished with a booming laugh.

"But Woodhouse; you have arranged a way to have him drop out of sight before the *Princess Mary* sails? There will be no confusion—no slip-up?"

"Do not fear," the physician reassured. "Everything will be arranged. His baggage will leave the Hotel Khedive for the dock to-morrow night; but it will not reach the dock. Yours——"

"Will be awaiting the transfer of tags at the Cap de Liberté—Mouquère's little place," the captain finished. "But the man himself— you're not thinking of mur——"

"My dear Nineteen Thirty-two," Doctor Koch interrupted, lifting protesting hands; "we do not use such crude methods; they are dangerous. The real Captain Woodhouse will not leave Alexandria—by sea, let us say—for many months. Although I have no doubt he will not be found in Alexandria the hour the *Princess Mary* sails. The papers he carries—the papers of identity and of transfer from Wady Halfa

to Gibraltar—will be in your hands in plenty
of time. You——"

The doctor stopped abruptly. A hidden
electric buzzer somewhere in the shadowed
room was clucking an alarm. Koch pressed a
button at the side of the operating chair.
There was a sound beyond closed doors of some
one passing through a hallway; the front door
opened and closed.

"Some one at the gate," Doctor Koch explained. "Cæsar, my playful little Numidian—
and an artist with the Bedouin dagger is
Cæsar—he goes to answer."

Their talk was desultory during the next
minutes. The doctor seemed restless under the
suspense of a pending announcement as to the
late visitor. Finally came a soft tapping on
the hidden door behind Woodhouse. The latter
heard the doctor exchange whispers with the
Numidian in the hallway. Finally, "Show him
into the waiting-room," Koch ordered. He
came back to where the captain was sitting, a
puzzled frown between his eyes.

"An Englishman, Cæsar says—an Englishman, who insists on seeing me—very import-

ant." Koch bit the end of one stubby thumb
in hurried thought. He suddenly whipped
open the door of one of the instrument cases,
pulled out a stethoscope, and hooked the two
little black receivers into his ears. Then he
turned to Woodhouse.

"Quick! Off with your coat and open your
shirt. You are a patient; I am just examining
you when interrupted. This may be one of
these clumsy English secret-service men, and I
might need your alibi." The sound of an opening door beyond the folding doors and of footsteps in the adjoining room.

"You say you are sleepless at night?"
Doctor Koch was talking English. "And you
have a temperature on arising? Hm'm! This
under your tongue, if you please"—he thrust a
clinical thermometer between Woodhouse's
lips; the latter already had his coat off, and was
unbuttoning his shirt. Koch gave him a meaning glance, and disappeared between the folding doors, closing them behind him.

The captain, feeling much like a fool with
the tiny glass tube sprouting from his lips, yet
with all his faculties strained to alertness,
awaited developments. If Doctor Koch's

hazard should prove correct and this was an English secret-service man come to arrest him, wouldn't suspicion also fall on whomever was found a visitor in the German spy's house? Arrest and search; examination of his scarab pin—that would not be pleasant.

He tried to hear what was being said beyond the folding doors, but could catch nothing save the deep rumble of the doctor's occasional bass and a higher, querulous voice raised in what might be argument. Had he dared, Woodhouse would have drawn closer to the crack in the folding doors so that he could hear what was passing; every instinct of self-preservation in him made his ears yearn to dissect this murmur into sense. But if Doctor Koch should catch him eavesdropping, embarrassment fatal to his plans might follow; besides, he had a feeling that eyes he could not see—perhaps the unwinking eyes of the Numidian, avid for an excuse to put into practise his dexterity with the Bedouin dagger—were on him.

Minutes slipped by. The captain still nursed the clinical thermometer. The mumble and muttering continued to sound through the closed doors. Suddenly the high whine of the

unseen visitor was raised in excitement. Came
clearly through to Woodhouse's ears his pas-
sionate declaration:

"But I tell you you've got to recognize me.
My number's Nineteen Thirty-two. My ticket
was stolen out of the head of my cane somewhere between Paris and Alexandria. But I
got it all right—got it from the Wilhelmstrasse
direct, with orders to report to Doctor Emil
Koch, in Alexandria!"

Capper! Capper, who was to be betrayed to
the firing squad in Malta, after his Wilhelmstrasse ticket had passed from his possession.
Capper on the job!

Woodhouse hurled every foot pound of his
will to hear into his ears. He caught Koch's
gruff answer:

"Young man, you're talking madness. You're
talking to a loyal British subject. I know
nothing about your Wilhelmstrasse or your
number. If I did not think you were drunk I'd
have you held here, to be turned over to the
military as a spy. Now, go before I change
my mind."

Again the querulous protestation of Capper,

met by the doctor's peremptory order. The
captain heard the front door close. A long
wait, and Doctor Koch's black beard, with the
surmounting eyes of thick glass, appeared at a
parting of the folding doors. Woodhouse, the
tiny thermometer still sticking absurdly from
his mouth, met the basilisk stare of those two
ovals of glass with a coldly casual glance. He
removed the thermometer from between his
lips and read it, with a smile, as if that were
part of playing a game. Still the ghastly stare
from the glass eyes over the bristling beard,
searching—searching.

"Well," Woodhouse said lightly, "no need of
an alibi evidently."

Doctor Koch stepped into the room with the
lightness of a cat, walked to a desk drawer at
one side, and fumbled there a second, his back
to his guest. When he turned he held a short-
barreled automatic at his hip; the muzzle covered the shirt-sleeved man in the chair.

"Much need—for an alibi—from you!"
Doctor Koch croaked, his voice dry and flat
with rage. "Much need, Mister Nineteen
Thirty-two. Commence your explanation im-

mediately, for this minute my temptation is
strong—very strong—to shoot you for the dog
you are."

"Is this—ah, customary?" Woodhouse
twiddled the tiny mercury tube between his
fingers and looked unflinchingly at the small
round mouth of the automatic. "Do you make
a practise of consulting a—friend with a revolver at your hip?"

"You heard—what was said in there!"
Koch's forehead was curiously ridged and
flushed with much blood.

"Did you ask me to listen? Surely, my dear
Doctor, you have provided doors that are sound-
proof. If I may suggest, isn't it about time
that you explain this—this melodrama?" The
captain's voice was cold; his lips were drawn
to a thin line. Koch's big head moved from side
to side with a gesture curiously like that of a
bull about to charge, but knowing not where
his enemy stands. He blurted out:

"For your information, if you did not over-
hear: An Englishman comes just now to ad-
dress me familiarly as of the Wilhelmstrasse.
He comes to say he was sent to report to me;
that his number in the Wilhelmstrasse is

nineteen thirty-two—nineteen thirty-two, remember; and I am to give him orders. Please
explain that before I pull this trigger."

"He showed you his number—his ticket,
then?" Woodhouse added this parenthetically.

"The man said his ticket had been stolen
from him some time after he left Paris—stolen
from the head of his cane, where he had it concealed. But the number was nineteen thirty-
two." The doctor voiced this last doggedly.

"You have, of course, had this man followed,"
the other put in. "You have not let him leave
this house alone."

"Cæsar was after him before he left the garden gate—naturally. But——"

Woodhouse held up an interrupting hand.

"Pardon me, Doctor Koch; did you get this
fellow's name?"

"He refused to give it—said I wouldn't know
him, anyway."

"Was he an undersized man, very thin,
sparse hair, and a face showing dissipation?"
Woodhouse went on. "Nervous, jerky way of
talking—fingers to his mouth, as if to feel his
words as they come out—brandy or wine
breath? Can't you guess who he was?"

"I guess nothing."

"The *target!*"

At the word Louisa had used in describing Capper to Woodhouse, Koch's face underwent a change. He lowered his pistol.

"*Ach!*" he said. "The man they are to arrest. And you have the number."

"That was Capper—Capper, formerly of the Belgian office—kicked out for drunkenness. One time he sold out Downing Street in the matter of the Lord Fisher letters; you remember the scandal when they came to light—his majesty, the kaiser's, Kiel speech referring to them. He is a good stalking horse."

Koch's suspicion had left him. Still gripping the automatic, he sat down on the edge of the operating chair, regarding the other man respectfully.

"Come—come, Doctor Koch; you and I can not continue longer at cross-purposes." The captain spoke with terse displeasure. "This man Capper showed you nothing to prove his claims, yet you come back to this room and threaten my life on the strength of a drunkard's bare word. What his mission is you know; how he got that number, which is the

number I have shown you on my ticket from
the Wilhelmstrasse—you understand how such
things are managed. I happen to know, however, because it was my business to know, that
Capper left Marseilles for Malta aboard *La
Vendée* four days ago; he was not expected to
go beyond Malta."

Koch caught him up: "But the fellow told
me his boat didn't stop at Malta—was warned
by wireless to proceed at all speed to Alexandria, for fear of the *Breslau,* known to be in
the Adriatic." Woodhouse spread out his
hands with a gesture of finality.

"There you are! Capper finds himself
stranded in Alexandria, knows somehow of
your position as a man of the Wilhelmstrasse—
such things can not be hid from the under-
ground workers; comes here to explain himself
to you and excuse himself for the loss of his
number. Is there anything more to be said
except that we must keep a close watch on
him?"

The physician rose and paced the room, his
hands clasped behind his back. The automatic
bobbed against the tails of his long coat as he
walked. After a minute's restless striding, he

broke his step before the desk, jerked open the drawer, and dropped the weapon in it. Back to where Woodhouse was sitting he stalked and held out his right hand stiffly.

"Your pardon, Number Nineteen Thirty-two! For my suspicion I apologize. But, you see my position—a very delicate one." Woodhouse rose, grasped the doctor's hand, and wrung it heartily.

"And now," he said, "to keep this fellow Capper in sight until the *Princess Mary* sails and I aboard her as Captain Woodhouse, of Wady Halfa. The man might trip us all up."

"He will not; be sure of that," Koch growled, helping Woodhouse into his coat and leading the way to the folding doors. "I will have Cæsar attend to him the minute he comes back to report where Capper is stopping."

"Until when?" the captain asked, pausing at the gate, to which Koch had escorted him.

"Here to-morrow night at nine," the doctor answered, and the gate shut behind him. Captain Woodhouse, alone under the shadowing trees of Queen's Terrace, drew in a long breath, shook his shoulders and started for the station and the midnight train to Alexandria.

CHAPTER V

CONSIDER the mental state of Mr. Billy Capper as he sank into a seat on the midnight suburban from Ramleh to Alexandria. Even to the guard, unused to particular observation of his passengers save as to their possible propensity for trying to beat their fares, the bundle of clothes surmounted by a rusty brown bowler which huddled under the sickly light of the second-class carriage bespoke either a candidate for a plunge off the quay or a "bloomer" returning from his wassailing. But the eyes of the man denied this latter hypothesis; sanity was in them, albeit the merciless sanity that refuses an alternative when fate has its victim pushed into a corner. So submerged was Capper under the flood of his own bitter cogitations that he had not noticed the other two passengers boarding the train at the little tiled station—a tall, quietly dressed white man and a Numidian with a cloak thrown over his white livery. The latter had faded like a shadow into the third-class carriage behind the one in which Capper rode.

Here was Capper—poor old Hardluck Billy Capper—floored again, and just when the tide of bad fortune was on the turn; so ran the minor strain of self-pity under the brown bowler. A failure once more, and through no fault of his own. No, no! Hadn't he been ready to deliver the goods? Hadn't he come all the way down here from Berlin, faithful to his pledge to Louisa, the girl in the Wilhelmstrasse, ready and willing to embark on that important mission of which he was to be told by Doctor Emil Koch? And what happens? Koch turns him into the street like a dog; threatens to have him before the military as a spy if he doesn't make himself scarce. Koch refuses even to admit he'd ever heard of the Wilhelmstrasse. Clever beggar! A jolly keen eye he's got for his own skin; won't take a chance on being betrayed into the hands of the English, even when he ought to see that a chap's honest when he comes and tells a straight story about losing that silly little bit of paper with his working number on it. What difference if he can't produce the ticket when he has the number pat on the tip of his tongue, and is willing to risk his own life to give that number to a stranger?

Back upon the old perplexity that had kept Capper's brain on strain ever since the first day aboard *La Vendée*—who had lifted his ticket, and when was it done? The man recalled, for the hundredth time, his awakening aboard the French liner—what a horror that first morning was, with the ratty little surgeon feeding a fellow aromatic spirits of ammonia like porridge! Capper, in this mood of detached review, saw himself painfully stretching out his arm from his bunk to grasp his stick the very first minute he was alone in the stateroom; the crooked handle comes off under his turning, and the white wisp of paper is stuck in the hollow of the stick. Blank paper!

Safe as safe could be had been that little square of paper Louisa had given him with his expense money, from the day he left Berlin until—when? To be sure, he had treated himself to a little of the grape in Paris and, maybe, in Marseilles; but his brain had been clear every minute. Oh, Capper would have sworn to that! The whole business of the disappearance of his Wilhelmstrasse ticket and the substitution of the blank was simply another low trick the Capper luck had played on him.

The train rushed through the dark toward the distant prickly coral bed of lights, and the whirligig of black despair churned under the brown bowler. No beginning, no end to the misery of it. Each new attempt to force a little light of hope into the blackness of his plight fetched up at the same dead wall—here was Billy Capper, hired by the Wilhelmstrasse, after having been booted out of the secret offices of England and Belgium—given a show for his white alley—and he couldn't move a hand to earn his new salary. Nor could he go back to Berlin, even though he dared return with confession of the stolen ticket; Berlin was no place for an Englishman right now, granting he could get there. No, he was in the backwash again—this time in this beastly half-caste city of Alexandria, and with—how much was it now?—with a beggarly fifteen pounds between himself and the beach.

Out of the ruck of Capper's sad reflections the old persistent call began to make itself heard before ever the train from Ramleh pulled into the Alexandria station. That elusive country of fountains, incense and rose dreams which can only be approached through the neck of a bottle spread itself before him alluringly, inviting him to forgetfulness. And Capper answered the call.

From the railroad station, he set his course through narrow villainous streets down to the district on Pharos, where the deep-water men of all the world gather to make vivid the nights of Egypt. Behind him was the faithful shadow, Cæsar, Doctor Koch's man. The Numidian trailed like a panther, slinking from cover to cover, bending his body as the big cat does to the accommodations of the trail's blinds.

Once Capper found himself in a blind alley, turned and strode out of it just in time to bump heavily into the unsuspected pursuer. Instantly a hem of the Numidian's cloak was lifted to screen his face, but not before the sharp eyes of the Englishman had seen and recognized it. A tart smile curled the corners of Capper's mouth as he passed on down the bazaar-lined street to the Tavern of Thermopylæ, at the next corner. So old Koch was taking precautions,

eh? Well, Capper, for one, could hardly blame
him; who wouldn't, under the circumstances?

The Tavern of Thermopylæ was built for
the Billy Cappers of the world—a place of
genial deviltry where every man's gold was
better than his name, and no man asked more
than to see the color of the stranger's money.
Here was gathered as sweet a company of as-
sassins as one could find from Port Said to
Honmoku, all gentle to fellows of their craft
under the freemasonry of hard liquor. Greeks,
Levantines, Liverpool lime-juicers from the
Cape, leech-eyed Finns from a Russian's stoke-
hole, tanned ivory runners from the forbidden
lands of the African back country—all that
made Tyre and Sidon infamous in Old Testa-
ment police records was represented there.

Capper called for an absinth dripper and established himself in a deserted corner of the
smoke-filled room. There was music, of sorts,
and singing; women whose eyes told strange
stories, and whose tongues jumped nimbly over
three or four languages, offered their com-
panionship to those who needed company with
their drink. But Billy Capper ignored the

music and closed his ears to the sirens; he knew
who was his best cup companion.

The thin green blood of the wormwood drip-
dripped down on to the ice in Capper's glass,
coloring it with a rime like moss. He watched
it, fascinated, and when he sipped the cold
sicky-sweet liquor he was eager as a child to
see how the pictures the absinth drew on the
ice had been changed by the draft. Sip—sip;
a soothing numbness came to the tortured
nerves. Sip—sip; the clouds of doubt and self-
pity pressing down on his brain began to shred
away. He saw things clearly now; everything
was sharp and clear as the point of an icicle.

He reviewed, with new zest, his recent ex-
periences, from the night he met Louisa in the
Café Riche up to his interview with Doctor
Koch. Louisa—that girl with the face of a fine
animal and a heart as cold as carved amethyst;
why had she been so willing to intercede for
Billy Capper with her superiors in the Wilhelmstrasse and procure him a number and a mission to Alexandria? For his information regarding the Anglo-Belgian understanding?
But she paid for that; the deal was fairly

closed with three hundred marks. Did Louisa
go further and list him in the Wilhelmstrasse
out of the goodness of her heart, or for old
memory's sake? Capper smiled wryly over his
absinth. There was no goodness in Louisa's
heart, and the strongest memory she had was
how nearly Billy Capper had dragged her down
with him in the scandal of the Lord Fisher
letters.

How the thin green blood of the wormwood
cleared the mind—made it leap to logical
reasoning!

Why had Louisa instructed him to leave
Marseilles by the steamer touching at Malta
when a swifter boat scheduled to go to Alexandria direct was leaving the French port a
few hours later? Was it that the girl intended
he should get no farther than Malta; that the
English there should——

Capper laughed like the philosopher who has
just discovered the absolute of life's futility.
The ticket—his ticket from the Wilhelmstrasse
which Louisa had procured for him; Louisa
wanted that for other purposes, and used him
as the dummy to obtain it. She wanted it before he could arrive at Malta—and she got it

before he left Marseilles. Even Louisa, the wise, had played without discounting the Double O on the wheel—fate's percentage in every game; she could not know the *Vendée* would be warned from lingering at Malta because of the exigency of war, and that Billy Capper would reach Alexandria, after all.

The green logic in the glass carried Capper along with mathematical exactness of deduction. As he sipped, his mind became a thing detached and, looking down from somewhere high above earth, reviewed the blundering course of Billy Capper's body from Berlin to Alexandria—the poor deluded body of a dupe. With this certitude of logic came the beginnings of resolve. Vague at first and intangible, then, helped by the absinth to focus, was this new determination. Capper nursed it, elaborated on it, took pleasure in forecasting its outcome, and viewing himself in the new light of a humble hero. It was near morning, and the Tavern of Thermopylæ was well-nigh deserted when Capper paid his score and blundered through the early-morning crowd of mixed races to his hotel. His legs were quite drunk, but his mind was coldly and acutely sober.

"Very drunk, master," was the report Cæsar, the Numidian, delivered to Doctor Koch at the Ramleh villa. The doctor, believing Cæsar to be a competent judge, chuckled in his beard. Cæsar was called off from the trail.

Across the street from Doctor Koch's home on Queen's Terrace was the summer home of a major of fusileers, whose station was up the Nile. But this summer it was not occupied. The major had hurried his family back to England at the first mutterings of the great war, and he himself had to stick by his regiment up in the doubtful Sudan country. Like Doctor Koch's place, the major's yard was surrounded by a high wall, over which the fronds of big palms and flowered shrubs draped themselves. The nearest villa, aside from the Kochs' across the street, was a hundred yards away. At night an arc light, set about thirty feet from Doctor Koch's gate, marked all the road thereabouts with sharp blocks of light and shadow. One lying close atop the wall about the major's yard, screened by the palms and the heavy branches of some night-blooming ghost flower, could command a perfect view of Doctor Koch's gateway without being himself visible.

At least, so Billy Capper found it on the night following his visit to the German physician's and his subsequent communion with himself at the Tavern of Thermopylæ. Almost with the falling of the dark, Capper had stepped off the train at Ramleh station, ferried himself by boat down the canal that passed behind the major's home, after careful reconnoitering, discovered that the tangle of wildwood about the house was not guarded by a watchman, and had so achieved his position of vantage on top of the wall directly opposite the gateway of No. 32. He was stretched flat. Through the spaces between the dry fingers of a palm leaf he could command a good view of the gate and of the road on either side. Few pedestrians passed below him; an automobile or two puffed by; but in the main, Queen's Terrace was deserted and Capper was alone. It was a tedious vigil. Capper had no reliance except his instinct of a spy familiar with spy's work to assure that he would be rewarded for his pains. Some sixth sense in him had prompted him to come thither, sure in the promise that the night would not be misspent. A clock somewhere off in the odorous dark struck the hour twice, and Capper fidgeted. The hard stone he was lying on cramped him.

The sound of footsteps on the flagged walk aroused momentary interest. He looked out through his screen of green and saw a tall well-knit figure of a man approach the opposite gate, stop and ring the bell. Instantly Capper tingled with the hunting fever of his trade. In the strong light from the arc he could study minutely the face of the man at the gate—smoothly shaven, slightly gaunt and with thin lips above a strong chin. It was a striking face—one easily remembered. The gate opened; beyond it Capper saw, for an instant, the white figure of the Numidian he had bumped into at the alley's mouth. The gate closed on both.

Another weary hour for the ferret on the wall, then something happened that was reward enough for cramped muscles and taut nerves. An automobile purred up to the gate; out of it hopped two men, while a third, tilted over like one drunk, remained on the rear seat of the tonneau. One rang the bell. The two before the gate fidgeted anxiously for it to be opened. Capper paid not so much heed to them as to the half-reclining figure in the machine. It was in strong light. Capper saw, with a leap of his heart, that the man in the machine was clothed in the khaki service uniform of the British army—an officer's uniform he judged by the trimness of its fitting, though he could not see the shoulder straps. The unconscious man was bareheaded and one side of his face was darkened by a broad trickle of blood from the scalp.

When the gate opened, there were a few hurried words between the Numidian and the two who had waited. All three united in lifting an inert figure from the car and carrying it quickly through the gate. Consumed with the desire to follow them into the labyrinth of the doctor's yard, yet not daring, Capper remained plastered to the wall.

Captain Woodhouse, sitting in the consultation room with the doctor, heard the front door open and the scuffle of burdened feet in the hall. Doctor Koch hopped nimbly to the folding doors and threw them back. First, the Numidian's broad back, then, the bent shoulders of two other men, both illy dressed, came into

view. Between them they carried the form
of a man in officer's khaki. Woodhouse could
not check a fluttering of the muscles in his
cheeks; this was a surprise to him; the doctor
had given no hint of it.

"Good—good!" clucked Koch, indicating that
they should lay their burden on the operating
chair. "Any trouble?"

"None in the least, Herr Doktor," the larger
of the two white men answered. "At the corner of the warehouse near the docks, where
it is dark—he was going early to the *Princess
Mary*, and ——"

"Yes, a tap on the head—so?" Koch broke
in, casting a quick glance toward where Captain Woodhouse had risen from his seat. A
shrewd appraising glance it was, which was
not lost on Woodhouse. He stepped forward
to join the physician by the side of the figure
on the operating chair.

"Our man, Doctor?" he queried casually.

"Your name sponsor," Koch answered, with
a satisfied chuckle; "the original Captain
Woodhouse of his majesty's signal service,
formerly stationed at Wady Halfa."

"Quite so," the other answered in English.
Doctor Koch clapped him on the shoulder.

"Perfect, man! You do the Englishman
from the book. It will fool them all."

Woodhouse shrugged his shoulders in depre-
cation. Koch cackled on, as he began to lay
out sponge and gauze bandages on the glass-
topped table by the operating chair:

"You see, I did not tell you of this because
—well, that fellow Capper's coming last night
looked bad; even your explanation did not altogether convince. So I thought we'd have this
little surprise for you. If you were an Englishman you'd show it in the face of this—
you couldn't help it. Eh?"

"Possibly not," the captain vouchsafed. "But
what is your plan, Doctor? What are you going to do with this Captain Woodhouse to
insure his being out of the way while I am in
Gibraltar. I hope no violence—unless necessary."

"Nothing more violent than a violent head-
ache and some fever," Koch answered. He
was busy fumbling in the unconscious man's
pockets. From the breast pocket of the uni-

form jacket he withdrew a wallet, glanced at its contents, and passed it to the captain.

"Your papers, Captain—the papers of transfer from Wady Halfa to Gibraltar. Money, too. I suppose we'll have to take that, also, to make appearances perfect—robbery following assault on the wharves."

Woodhouse pocketed the military papers in the wallet and laid it down, the money untouched. The two white aids of Doctor Koch, who were standing by the folding doors, eyed the leather folder hungrily. Koch, meanwhile, had stripped off the jacket from the Englishman and was rolling up the right sleeve of his shirt. That done, he brought down from the top of the glass instrument case a wooden rack containing several test tubes, stoppled with cotton. One glass tube he lifted out of the rack and squinted at its clouded contents against the light.

"A very handy little thing—very handy." Koch was talking to himself as much as to Woodhouse. "A sweet little product of the Niam Niam country down in Belgian Kongo. Natives think no more of it than they would

of a water fly's bite; but the white man
is——"

"A virus of some kind?" the other guessed.

"Of my own isolation," Doctor Koch answered proudly. He scraped the skin on the
victim's arm until the blood came, then dipped
an ivory spatula into the tube of murky gelatine and transferred what it brought up to the
raw place in the flesh.

"The action is very quick, and may be violent," he continued. "Our friend here won't
recover consciousness for three days, and he
will be unable to stand on his feet for two
weeks, at least—dizziness, intermittent fever,
clouded memory; he'll be pretty sick."

"But not too sick to communicate with
others," Woodhouse suggested. "Surely——"

"Maybe not too sick, but unable to communicate with others," Doctor Koch interrupted,
with a booming laugh. "This time to-morrow
night our friend will be well out on the Libyan
Desert, with some ungentle Bedouins for company. He's bound for Fezzan—and it will be
a long way home without money. Who knows?
Maybe three months."

Very deftly Koch bound up the abrasion on the Englishman's arm with gauze, explaining as he worked that the man's desert guardians would have instructions to remove the bandages before he recovered his faculties. There would be nothing to tell the luckless prisoner more than that he had been kidnaped, robbed and carried away by tribesmen—a not uncommon occurrence in lower Egypt. Koch completed his work by directing his aids to strip off the rest of the unconscious man's uniform and clothe him in a nondescript civilian garb that Cæsar brought into the consultation room from the mysterious upper regions of the house.

"Exit Captain Woodhouse of the signal service," the smiling doctor exclaimed when the last button of the misfit jacket had been flipped into its buttonhole, "and enter Captain Woodhouse of the Wilhelmstrasse." Turning, he bowed humorously to the lean-faced man beside him. He nodded his head at Cæsar; the latter dived into a cupboard at the far end of the room and brought out a squat flask and glasses, which he passed around. When the liquor had been poured, Doctor Koch lifted his glass and squinted through it with the air of a gentle satyr.

"Gentlemen, we drink to what will happen soon on the Rock of Gibraltar!" All downed the toast gravely. Then the master of the house jerked his head toward the unconscious man on the operating chair. Cæsar and the two white men lifted the limp body and started with it to the door, Doctor Koch preceding them to open doors. The muffled chug-chugging of the auto at the gate sounded almost at once.

The doctor and Number Nineteen Thirty-two remained together in the consultation room for a few minutes, going over, in final review, the plans that the latter was to put into execution at the great English stronghold on the Rock. The captain looked at his watch, found the hour late, and rose to depart. Doctor Koch accompanied him to the gate, and stood with him for a minute under the strong light from the near-by arc.

"You go direct to the *Princess Mary?*" he asked.

"Direct to the *Princess Mary*," the other answered. "She is to sail at five o'clock."

"Then God guard you, my friend, on—your great adventure." They clasped hands, and the gate closed behind the doctor.

A shadow skipped from the top of the wall about the major's house across the road. A shadow dogged the footsteps of the tall well-knit man who strode down the deserted Queen's Terrace toward the tiled station by the tracks. A little more than an hour later, the same shadow flitted up the gangplank of the *Princess Mary* at her berth. When the big P. & O. liner pulled out at dawn, she carried among her saloon passengers one registered as "C. G. Woodhouse, Capt. Sig. Service," and in her second cabin a "William Capper."

CHAPTER VI

A FUGITIVE

"**N**O, madam does not know me; but she must see me. Oh, I know she will see me. Tell her, please, it is a girl from New York all alone in Paris who needs her help."

The butler looked again at the card the visitor had given him. Quick suspicion flashed into his tired eyes—the same suspicion that had all Paris mad.

"Ger-son — Mademoiselle Ger-son. That name, excuse me, if I say it—that name ees——"

"It sounds German; yes. Haven't I had that told me a thousand times these last few days?" The girl's shoulders drooped limply, and she tried to smile, but somehow failed. "But it's my name, and I'm an American—been an American twenty-two years. Please—please!"

"Madam the ambassador's wife; she ees overwhelm wiz woark." The butler gave the door an insinuating push. Jane Gerson's patent-leather boot stopped it. She made a quick rummage in her bag, and when she withdrew her hand, a bit of bank paper crinkled in it. The butler pocketed the note with perfect legerdemain, smiled a formal thanks and invited Jane into the dark cool hallway of the embassy. She dropped on a skin-covered couch, utterly spent. Hours she had passed moving, foot by foot, in an interminable line, up to a little wicket in a steamship office, only to be told, "Every boat's sold out." Other grilling hours she had passed similarly before the express office, to find, at last, that her little paper booklet of checks was as worthless as a steamship folder. Food even lacked, because the money she offered was not acceptable. For a week she had lived in the seething caldron that was Paris in war time, harried, buffeted, trampled and stampeded—a chip on the froth of madness. This day, the third of August, found Jane Gerson summoning the last remnants of her flagging nerve to the supreme endeavor. Upon her visit to the embassy depended everything: her safety, the future she was battling for. But now, with the first barrier passed, she found herself suddenly faint and weak.

"Madam the ambassador's wife will see you. Come!" The butler's voice sounded from afar off, though Jane saw the gleaming buckles at his knees very close. The pounding of her heart almost choked her as she rose to follow him. Down a long hall and into a richly furnished drawing-room, now strangely transformed by the presence of desks, filing cabinets, and busy girl stenographers; the click of typewriters and rustle of papers gave the air of an office at top pressure. The butler showed Jane to a couch near the portières and withdrew. From the tangle of desks at the opposite end of the room, a woman with a kindly face crossed, with hand extended. Jane rose, grasped the hand and squeezed convulsively.

"You are——"

"Yes, my dear, I am the wife of the ambassador. Be seated and tell me all your troubles. We are pretty busy here, but not too busy to help—if we can."

Jane looked into the sympathetic eyes of the ambassador's wife, and what she found there was like a draft of water to her parched soul. The elder woman, smiling down into the white face, wherein the large brown eyes burned unnaturally bright, saw a trembling of the lips instantly conquered by a rallying will, and she patted the small hand hearteningly.

"Dear lady," Jane began, almost as a little child, "I must get out of Paris, and I've come to you to help me. Every way is closed except through you."

"So many hundreds like you, poor girl. All want to get back to the home country, and we are so helpless to aid every one." The lady of the embassy thought, as she cast a swift glance over the slender shoulders and diminutive figure beneath them, that here, indeed, was a babe in the woods. The blatant, self-assured tourist demanding assistance from her country's representative as a right she knew; also the shifty, sloe-eyed demi-vierge who wanted no questions asked. But such a one as this little person——

"You see, I am a buyer for Hildebrand's store in New York." Jane was rushing breathlessly to the heart of her tragedy. "This is my very first trip as buyer, and—it will be my last unless I can get through the lines and back to New York. I have seventy of the very last gowns from Poiret, from Paquin and Worth— you know what they will mean in the old town back home—and I must—just simply *must* get them through. You understand! With them, Hildebrand can crow over every other gown shop in New York. He can be supreme, and I will be—well, I will be made!"

The kindly eyes were still smiling, and the woman's heart, which is unchanged even in the breast of an ambassador's wife, was leaping to the magic lure of that simple word— gowns.

"But—but the banks refuse to give me a cent on my letter of credit. The express office says my checks, which I brought along for incidentals, can not be cashed. The steamship companies will not sell a berth in the steerage, even, out of Havre or Antwerp or Southampton—everything gobbled up. You can't get trunks on an aeroplane, or I'd try that. I just don't know where to turn, and so I've come to you. You must know some way out."

Jane unconsciously clasped her hands in supplication, and upon her face, flushed now with

the warmth of her pleading, was the dawning
of hope. It was as if the girl were assured
that once the ambassador's wife heard her
story, by some magic she could solve the difficulties. The older woman read this trust, and
was touched by it.

"Have you thought of catching a boat at
Gibraltar?" she asked. "They are not so
crowded; people haven't begun to rush out of
Italy yet."

"But nobody will honor my letter of credit,"
Jane mourned. "And, besides, all the trains
south of Paris are given up to the mobiliza-
tion. Nobody can ride on them but soldiers."
The lady of the embassy knit her brows for a
few minutes while Jane anxiously scanned her
face. Finally she spoke:

"The ambassador knows a gentleman—a
large-hearted American gentleman here in
Paris—who has promised his willingness to
help in deserving cases by advancing money
on letters of credit. And with money there is
a way—just a possible way—of getting to
Gibraltar. Leave your letter of credit with
me, my dear; go to the police station in the
district where you live and get your pass

through the lines, just as a precaution against the possibility of your being able to leave to-night. Then come back here and see me at four o'clock. Perhaps—just a chance——"

Hildebrand's buyer seized the hands of the embassy's lady ecstatically, tumbled words of thanks crowding to her lips. When she went out into the street, the sun was shining as it had not shone for her for a dreary terrible week.

At seven o'clock that night a big Roman-nosed automobile, long and low and powerful as a torpedo on wheels, pulled up at the door of the American embassy. Two bulky osier baskets were strapped on the back of its ton-neau; in the rear seat were many rugs. A young chap with a sharp shrewd face—an American—sat behind the wheel.

The door of the embassy opened, and Jane Gerson, swathed in veils, and with a gray duster buttoned tight about her, danced out; behind her followed the ambassador, the lady of the embassy and a bevy of girls, the volun-teer aids of the overworked representative's staff. Jane's arms went about the ambassa-dor's wife in an impulsive hug of gratitude and good-by; the ambassador received a hearty handshake for his "God speed you!" A waving of hands and fluttering of handkerchiefs, and the car leaped forward. Jane Gerson leaned far over the back, and, through cupped hands, she shouted: "I'll paint Hildebrand's sign on the Rock of Gibraltar!"

Over bridges and through outlying faubourgs sped the car until the Barrier was gained. There crossed bayonets denying passage, an officer with a pocket flash pawing over pass and passport, a curt dismissal, and once more the motor purred its speed song, and the lights of the road flashed by. More picket lines, more sprouting of armed men from the dark, and flashing of lights upon official signatures. On the heights appeared the hump-shouldered bastions of the great outer forts, squatting like huge fighting beasts of the night, ready to spring upon the invader. Bugles sounded; the white arms of search-lights swung back and forth across the arc of night in their ceaseless calisthenics; a murmuring and stamping of many men and beasts was everywhere.

The ultimate picket line gained and passed, the car leaped forward with the bound of some freed animal, its twin headlights feeling far ahead the road to the south. Behind lay Paris, the city of dread. Ahead—far ahead, where the continent is spiked down with a rock, Gibraltar. Beyond that the safe haven from this madness of the millions—America.

Jane Gerson stretched out her arms to the vision and laughed shrilly.

CHAPTER VII

THE HOTEL SPLENDIDE

MR. JOSEPH ALMER, proprietor of the Hotel Splendide, on Gibraltar's Waterport Street, was alone in his office, busy over his books. The day was August fifth. The night before the cable had flashed word to General Sir George Crandall, Governor-general of the Rock, that England had hurled herself into the great war. But that was no concern of Mr. Joseph Almer except as it affected the hotel business; admittedly it did bring complications there.

A sleek well-fed Swiss he was; one whose neutrality was publicly as impervious as the rocky barriers of his home land. A bland eye and a suave professional smile were the ever-present advertisements of urbanity on Joseph Almer's chubby countenance. He spoke with an accent that might have got him into trouble with the English masters of the Rock had they not known that certain cantons in Switzerland occupy an unfortunate contiguity with Germany, and Almer, therefore, was hardly to be blamed for an accident of birth. From a window of his office, he looked out on crooked Waterport Street, where all the world of the Mediterranean shuffled by on shoes, slippers and bare feet. Just across his desk was the Hotel Splendide's reception room—a sad retreat, wherein a superannuated parlor set of worn red plush tried to give the lie to the reflection cast back at it by the dingy gold-framed mirror over the battered fireplace. Gaudy steamship posters and lithographs of the Sphinx and kindred tourists' delights were the walls' only decorations. Not even the potted palm, which is the hotel man's cure-all, was there to screen the interior of the office-reception room from the curious eyes of the street, just beyond swinging glass doors. Joseph Almer had taken poetic license with the word "splendide"; but in Gibraltar that is permissible; necessary, in fact. Little there lives up to its reputation save the Rock itself.

It was four in the afternoon. The street outside steamed with heat, and the odors that make Gibraltar a lasting memory were at their

prime of distillation. The proprietor of the
Splendide was nodding over his books. A light
footfall on the boards beyond the desk roused
him. A girl with two cigar boxes under her
arm slipped, like a shadow, up to the desk. She
was dressed in the bright colors of Spain,
claret-colored skirt under a broad Romany
sash, and with thin white waist, open at rounded throat. A cheap tortoise-shell comb held her
coils of chestnut hair high on her head. Louisa
of the Wilhelmstrasse; but not the same Louisa
—the sophisticated Louisa of the Café Riche
and the Winter Garden. A timid little cigar
maker she was, here in Gibraltar.

"Louisa!" Almer's head bobbed up on a suddenly stiffened neck as he whispered her name.
She set her boxes of cigars on the desk, opened
them, and as she made gestures to point the
worthiness of her wares, she spoke swiftly, and
in a half whisper:

"All is as we hoped, Almer. He comes on
the *Princess Mary*—a cablegram from Koch
just got through to-day. I wanted——"

"You mean——" Almer thrust his head forward in his eagerness, and his eyes were bright
beads.

"Captain Woodhouse—our Captain Woodhouse!" The girl's voice trembled in exultation. "And his number—his Wilhelmstrasse number—is—listen carefully: Nineteen Thirtytwo."

"Nineteen Thirty-two," Almer repeated, under his breath. Then aloud: "On the *Princess Mary*, you say?"

"Yes; she is already anchored in the straits. The tenders are coming ashore. He will come here, for such were his directions in Alexandria." Louisa started to move toward the street door.

"But you," Almer stopped her; "the English are making a round-up of suspects on the Rock. They will ask questions—perhaps arrest——"

"Me? No, I think not. Just because I was away from Gibraltar for six weeks and have returned so recently is not enough to rouse suspicion. Haven't I been Josepha, the cigar girl, to every Tommy in the garrison for nearly a year? No—no, señor; you are wrong. These are the purest cigars made south of Madrid. Indeed, señor."

The girl had suddenly changed her tone to

one of professional wheedling, for she saw
three entering the door. Almer lifted his voice
angrily:

"Josepha, your mother is substituting with
these cigars. Take them back and tell her if
I catch her doing this again it means the cells
for her."

The cigar girl bowed her head in simulated
fright, sped past the incoming tourists, and
lost herself in the shifting crowd on the street.
Almer permitted himself to mutter angrily as
he turned back to his books.

"You see, mother? See that hotel keeper
lose his temper and tongue-lash that poor girl?
Just what I tell you—these foreigners don't
know how to be polite to ladies."

Henry J. Sherman—"yes, sir, of Kewanee,
Illynoy"—mopped his bald pink dome and
glared truculently at the insulting back of Joseph Almer. Mrs. Sherman, the lady of direct
impulses who had contrived to stare Captain
Woodhouse out of countenance in the Winter
Garden not long back, cast herself despondent-
ly on the decrepit lounge and appeared to need
little invitation to be precipitated into a cry-

"Haven't I been Josepha for nearly a year?"

ing spell. Her daughter Kitty, a winsome little slip, stood behind her, arms about the mother's neck, and her hands stroking the maternal cheeks.

"There—there, mother; everything'll come out right," Kitty vaguely assured. Mrs. Sherman, determined to have no eye for the cloud's silver lining, rocked back and forth on the sofa and gave voice to her woe:

"Oh, we'll never see Kewanee again. I know it! I know it! With everybody pushing and shoving us away from the steamers— everybody refusing to cash our checks, and all this fighting going on somewhere up among the Belgians——" The lady from Kewanee pulled out the stopper of her grief, and the tears came copiously. Mr. Sherman, who had made an elaborate pretense of studying a steamer guide he found on the table, looked up hurriedly and blew his nose loudly in sympathy.

"Cheer up, mother. Even if this first trip of ours—this 'Grand Tower,' as the guide-books call it—has been sorta tough, we had one compensation anyway. We saw the Palace of

Peace at the Hague before the war broke out. Guess they're leasing it for a skating rink now, though."

"How can you joke when we're in such a fix? He-Henry, you ne-never do take things seriously!"

"Why not joke, mother? Only thing you can do over here you don't have to pay for. Cheer up! There's the *Saxonia* due here from Naples some time soon. Maybe we can horn a way up her gangplank. Consul says——"

Mrs. Sherman looked up from her handkerchief with withering scorn.

"Tell me a way we can get aboard *any* ship without having the money to pay our passage. Tell me that, Henry Sherman!"

"Well, we've been broke before, mother," her spouse answered cheerily, rocking himself on heels and toes. "Remember when we were first married and had that little house on Liberty Street—the newest house in Kewanee it was; and we didn't have a hired girl, then, mother. But we come out all right, didn't we?" He patted his daughter's shoulder and winked ponderously. "Come on, girls and boys, we'll go look over those Rock Chambers the English hollowed out. We can't sit in our room and mope all day."

The gentleman who knew Kewanee was making for the door when Almer, the suave, came out from behind his desk and stopped him with a warning hand.

"I am afraid the gentleman can not see the famous Rock Chambers," he purred. "This is war time—since yesterday, you know. Tourists are not allowed in the fortifications."

"Like to see who'd stop me!" Henry J. Sherman drew himself up to his full five feet seven and frowned at the Swiss. Almer rubbed his hands.

"A soldier—with a gun, most probably, sir."

Mrs. Sherman rose and hurried to her husband's side, in alarm.

"Henry—Henry! Don't you go and get arrested again! Remember that last time—the Frenchman at that Bordeaux town." Sherman allowed discretion to soften his valor.

"Well, anyway"—he turned again to the proprietor—"they'll let us see that famous signal tower up on top of the Rock. Mother, they say from that tower up there, they can keep tabs on a ship sixty miles away. Fellow down at the consulate was telling me just this morning that's the king-pin of the whole works. Harbor's full of mines and things; electric switch in the signal tower. Press a switch up there, and everything in the harbor—Blam!" He shot his hands above his head to denote the cataclysm. Almer smiled sardonically and drew the Illinois citizen to one side.

"I would give you a piece of advice," he said in a low voice. "It is——"

"Say, proprietor; you don't charge for advice, do you?" Sherman regarded him quizzically.

"It is this," Almer went on, unperturbed: "If I were you I would not talk much about the fortifications of the Rock. Even talk is— ah—dangerous if too much indulged."

"Huh! I guess you're right," said Sherman thoughtfully. "You see—we don't know much about diplomacy out where I come from. Though that ain't stopping any of the Democrats from going abroad in the Diplomatic Service as fast as Bryan'll take 'em."

Interruption came startlingly. A sergeant and three soldiers with guns swung through the open doors from Waterport Street. Gun butts struck the floor with a heavy thud. The sergeant stepped forward and saluted Almer with a businesslike sweep of hand to visor.

"See here, landlord!" the sergeant spoke up briskly. "Fritz, the barber, lives here, does he not?" Almer nodded. "We want him. Find him in the barber shop, eh?"

The sergeant turned and gave directions to the guard. They tramped through a swinging door by the side of the desk while the Shermans, parents and daughter alike, looked on, with round eyes. In less than a minute, the men in khaki returned, escorting a quaking man in white jacket. The barber, greatly flustered, protested in English strongly reminiscent of his fatherland.

"Orders to take you, Fritz," the sergeant explained not unkindly.

"But I haf done nothing," the barber cried. "For ten years I haf shaved you. You know I am a harmless old German." The sergeant shrugged.

"I fancy they think you are working for the

Wilhelmstrasse, Fritz, and they want to have
you where they can keep their eyes on you.
Sorry, you know."

The free-born instincts of Henry J. Sherman
would not be downed longer. He had wit-
nessed the little tragedy of the German barber
with growing ire, and now he stepped up to
the sergeant truculently.

"Seems to me you're not giving Fritz here
a square deal, if you want to know what I
think," he blustered. "Now, in my country——" The sergeant turned on him sharply.

"Who are you—and what are you doing in
Gib?" he snapped. A moan from Mrs. Sherman, who threw herself in her daughter's
arms.

"Kitty, your father's gone and got himself
arrested again!"

"Who am I?" Sherman echoed with dignity.
"My name, young fellow, is Henry J. Sher-
man, and I live in Kewanee, Illynoy. I'm an
American citizen, and you can't——"

"Your passports—quick!" The sergeant
held out his hand imperiously.

"Oh, that's all right, young fellow; I've got
'em, all right." Kewanee's leading light be-

"Who are you?" snapped the sergeant.

gan to fumble in the spacious breast pocket of
his long-tailed coat. As he groped through a
packet of papers and letters, he kept up a running fire of comment and exposition:

"Had 'em this afternoon, all right. Here;
no, that's my letter of credit. It would buy
Main Street at home, but I can't get a ham
sandwich on it here. This is—no; that's my
only son's little girl, Emmaline, taken the
day she was four years old. Fancy little girl,
eh? Now, that's funny I can't—here's that
list of geegaws I was to buy for my partner
in the Empire Mills, flour and buckwheat.
Guess he'll have to whistle for 'em. Now don't
get impatient, young fellow. This—— Land's
sakes, mother, that letter you gave me to mail,
in Algy-kiras—— Ah, here you are, all proper
and scientific enough as passports go, I guess."

The sergeant whisked the heavily creased
document from Sherman's hand, scanned it
hastily, and gave it back, without a word. The
outraged American tucked up his chin and gave
the sergeant glare for glare.

"If you ever come to Kewanee, young fellow," he snorted. "I'll be happy to show you
our new jail."

"Close in! March!" commanded the sergeant. The guard surrounded the hapless barber and wheeled through the door, their guns hedging his white jacket about inexorably. Sherman's hands spread his coat tails wide apart, and he rocked back and forth on heels and toes, his eyes smoldering.

"Come on, father"—Kitty had slipped her hand through her dad's arm, and was imparting direct strategy in a low voice—"we'll take mother down the street to look at the shops and make her forget our troubles. They've got some wonderful Moroccan bazaars in town; Baedeker says so."

"Shops, did you say?" Mrs. Sherman perked up at once, forgetting her grief under the superior lure.

"Yes, mother. Come on, let's go down and look 'em over." Sherman's good humor was quite restored. He pinched Kitty's arm in compliment for her guile. "Maybe they'll let us look at their stuff without charging anything; but we couldn't buy a postage stamp, remember."

They sailed out into the crowded street and

lost themselves amid the scourings of Africa and south Europe. Almer was alone in the office.

The proprietor fidgeted. He walked to the door and looked down the street in the direction of the quays. He pulled his watch from his pocket and compared it with the blue face of the Dutch clock on the wall. His pudgy hands clasped and unclasped themselves behind his back nervously. An Arab hotel porter and runner at the docks came swinging through the front door with a small steamer trunk on his shoulders, and Almer started forward expectantly. Behind the porter came a tall well-knit man, dressed in quiet traveling suit—the Captain Woodhouse who had sailed from Alexandria as a passenger aboard the *Princess Mary*.

He paused for an instant as his eyes met those of the proprietor. Almer bowed and hastened behind the desk. Woodhouse stepped up to the register and scanned it casually.

"A room, sir?" Almer held out a pen invitingly.

"For the night, yes," Woodhouse answered

shortly, and he signed the register. Almer's eyes followed the strokes of the pen eagerly.

"Ah, from Egypt, Captain? You were aboard the *Princess Mary*, then?"

"From Alexandria, yes. Show me my room, please. Beastly tired."

The Arab porter darted forward, and Woodhouse was turning to follow him when he nearly collided with a man just entering the street door. It was Mr. Billy Capper.

Both recoiled as their eyes met. Just the faintest flicker of surprise, instantly suppressed, tightened the muscles of the captain's jaws. He murmured a "Beg pardon" and started to pass. Capper deliberately set himself in the other's path and, with a wry smile, held out his hand.

"Captain Woodhouse, I believe." Capper put a tang of sarcasm, corroding as acid, into the words. He was still smiling. The other man drew back and eyed him coldly.

"I do not know you. Some mistake," Woodhouse said.

Almer was moving around from behind the desk with the soft tread of a cat, his eyes fixed on the hard-bitten face of Capper.

"Hah! Don't recognize the second-cabin passengers aboard the *Princess Mary*, eh?" Capper sneered. "Little bit discriminating that way, eh? Well, my name's Capper—Mr. William Capper. Never heard the name—in Alexandria; what?"

"You are drunk. Stand aside!" Woodhouse spoke quietly; his face was very white and strained. Almer launched himself suddenly between the two and laid his hands roughly on Capper's thin shoulders.

"Out you go!" he choked in a thick guttural. "I'll have no loafer insulting guests in my house."

"Oh, you won't, won't you? But supposing I want to take a room here—pay you good English gold for it. You'll sing a different tune, then."

"Before I throw you out, kindly leave my place." By a quick turn, Almer had Capper facing the door; his grip was iron. The smaller man tried to walk to the door with dignity. There he paused and looked back over his shoulder.

"Remember, Captain Woodhouse," he called back. "Remember the name against the time we'll meet again. Capper—Mr. William Capper."

Capper disappeared. Almer came back to begin profuse apologies to his guest. Woodhouse was coolly lighting a cigarette. Their eyes met.

CHAPTER VIII

CHAFF OF WAR

DINNER that evening in the faded dining-room of the Hotel Splendide was in the way of being a doleful affair for the folk from Kewanee, aside from Captain Woodhouse, the only persons at table there. Woodhouse, true to the continental tradition of exclusiveness, had isolated himself against possible approach by sitting at the table farthest from the Shermans; his back presented an uncompromising denial of fraternity. As for Mrs. Sherman, the afternoon's visit to the bazaars had been anything but a solace, emphasizing, as it did, their grievous poverty in the midst of a plenty contemptuous of a mere letter of credit. Henry J. was wallowing in the lowest depths of nostalgia; he tortured himself with the reflection that this was lodge night in Kewanee and he would not be sitting in his chair. Miss Kitty contemplated with melancholy the distress of her parents.

A tall slender youth with tired eyes and affecting the blasé slouch of the boulevards appeared in the door and cast about for a choice of tables. Him Mr. Sherman impaled with a glance of disapproval which suddenly changed to wondering recognition. He dropped his fork and jumped to his feet.

"Bless me, mother, if it isn't Willy Kimball from old Kewanee!" Sherman waved his napkin at the young man, summoning him in the name of Kewanee to come and meet the home folks. The tired eyes lighted perceptibly, and a lukewarm smile played about Mr. Kimball's effeminate mouth as he stepped up to the table.

"Why, Mrs. Sherman—and Kitty! And you, Mr. Sherman—charmed!" He accepted the proffered seat by the side of Kitty, receiving their hearty hails with languid politeness. With the sureness of English restraint, Mr. Willy Kimball refused to become excited. He was of the type of exotic Americans who try to forget grandpa's corn-fed hogs and grandma's hand-churned butter. His speech was of Rotten Row and his clothes Piccadilly.

"Terrible business, this!" The youth fluttered his hands feebly. "All this harrying about and peeping at passports by every silly officer one meets. I'm afraid I'll have to go over to America until it's all over—on my way now, in fact."

"Afraid!" Sherman sniffed loudly, and appraised Mr. Kimball's tailoring with a disapproving eye. "Well, Willy, it would be too bad if you had to go back to Kewanee after your many years in Paris, France; now, wouldn't it?"

Kimball turned to the women for sympathy. "Reserved a compartment to come down from Paris. Beastly treatment. Held up at every city—other people crowded in my apartment, though I'd paid to have it alone, of course—soldier chap comes along and seizes my valet and makes him join the colors and all that sort——"

"Huh! Your father managed to worry along without a val-lay, and he was respected in Kewanee." This in disgust from Henry J.

Kitty flashed a reproving glance at her father and deftly turned the expatriate into a recounting of his adventures. Under her unaffected lead the youth, who shuddered inwardly at the appellation of "Willy," thawed considerably, and soon there was an animated swapping of reminiscences of the Great Terror —hours on end before the banks and express offices, dodging of police impositions, scrambling for steamer accommodations—all that went to compose the refugee Americans' great epic of August, 1914.

Sherman took pride in his superior adventures: "Five times arrested between Berlin and Gibraltar, and what I said to that Dutchman on the Swiss frontier was enough to make his hair curl."

"Tell you what, Willy: you come on back to Kewanee with us, and mother and you'll lecture before the Thursday Afternoon Ladies' Literary Club," Sherman boomed, with a hearty blow of the hand between Willy's shoulder blades. "I'll have Ed Porter announce it in advance in the *Daily Enterprise,* and we'll have the whole town there to listen. 'Ezra Kimball's Boy Tells Thrilling Tale of War's Alarms.' That's the way the head-lines'll read in the *Enterprise* next week."

The expatriate shivered and tried to smile.

"We'll let mother do the lecturing," Kitty came to his rescue. " 'How to Live in Europe on a Letter of Discredit.' That will have all the gossips of Kewanee buzzing, mother."

The meal drew to a close happily in contrast to its beginning. Mrs. Sherman and her daughter rose to pass out into the reception room. Sherman and Kimball lingered.

"Ah-h, Willy——"

"Mr. Sherman——"

Both began in unison, each somewhat furtive and shamefaced.

"Have you any money?" The queries were voiced as one. For an instant confusion; then the older man looked up into the younger's face —a bit flushed it was—and guffawed.

"Not a postage stamp, Willy! I guess we're both beggars, and if mother and Kitty didn't have five trunks between them this Swiss holdup man who says he's proprietor of this way-station hotel wouldn't trust us for a fried egg."

"Same here," admitted Kimball. "I'm badly bent."

"They can't keep us down—us Americans!" Sherman cheered, taking the youth's arm and piloting him out into the reception room. "We'll find a way out if we have to cable for a warship to come and get us."

Just as Sherman and Kimball emerged from
the dining-room, there was a diversion out beyond the glass doors on Waterport Street. A
small cart drew up; from its seat jumped a
young woman in a duster and with a heavy
automobile veil swathed under her chin. To
the Arab porter who had bounded out to the
street she gave directions for the removal from
the cart of her baggage, two heavy suit-cases
and two ponderous osier baskets. These latter
she was particularly tender of, following them
into the hotel's reception room and directing
where they should be put before the desk.

The newcomer was Jane Gerson, Hildebrand's buyer, at the end of her gasoline flight
from Paris. Cool, capable, self-reliant as on
the night she saw the bastions of the capital's
outer forts fade under the white spikes of the
search-lights, Jane strode up the desk to face
the smiling Almer.

"Is this a fortress or a hotel?" she challenged.

"A hotel, lady, a hotel," Almer purred. "A
nice room—yes. Will the lady be with us
long?"

"Heaven forbid! The lady is going to be

on the first ship leaving for New York. And
if there are no ships, I'll look over the stock
of coal barges you have in your harbor." She
seized a pen and dashed her signature on the
register. The Shermans had pricked up their
ears at the newcomer's first words. Now
Henry J. pressed forward, his face glowing
welcome.

"An American—a simon-pure citizen of the
United States—I thought so. Welcome to the
little old Rock!" He took both the girl's hands
impulsively and pumped them. Mrs. Sherman,
Kitty and Willy Kimball crowded around, and
the clatter of voices was instantaneous: "By
auto from Paris; goodness me!" "Not a thing
to eat for three days but rye bread!" "From
Strassburg to Luneville in a farmer's wagon!"
Each in a whirlwind of ejaculation tried to
outdo the other's story of hardship and priva-
tion.

The front doors opened again, and the sergeant and guard who had earlier carried off
Fritz, the barber, entered. Again gun butts
thumped ominously. Jane looked over her
shoulder at the khaki-coated men, and confided
in the Shermans:

"I think that man's been following me ever since I landed from the ferry."

"I have," answered the sergeant, stepping briskly forward and saluting. "You are a stranger on the Rock. You come here from——"

"From Paris, by motor, to the town across the bay; then over here on the ferry," the girl answered promptly. "What about it?"

"Your name?"

"Jane Gerson. Yes, yes, it sounds German, I know. But that's not my fault. I'm an American—a red-hot American, too, for the last two weeks."

The sergeant's face was wooden.

"Where are you going?"

"To New York, on the *Saxonia*, just as soon as I can. And the British army can't stop me."

"Indeed!" The sergeant permitted himself a fleeting smile. "From Paris by motor, eh? Your passports, please."

"I haven't any," Jane retorted, with a shade of defiance. "They were taken from me in Spain, just over the French border, and were not returned."

The sergeant raised his eyebrows in surprise not unmixed with irony. He pointed to the two big osier baskets, demanding to know what they contained.

"Gowns—the last gowns made in Paris before the crash. Fashion's last gasp. I am a buyer of gowns for Hildebrand's store in New York."

Ecstatic gurgles of pleasure from Mrs. Sherman and her daughter greeted this announcement. They pressed about the baskets and regarded them lovingly.

The sergeant pushed them away and tried to throw back the covers.

"Open your baggage—all of it!" he commanded snappishly.

Jane, explaining over her shoulder to the women, stooped to fumble with the hasps.

"Seventy of the darlingest gowns—the very last Paul Poiret and Paquin and Worth made before they closed shop and marched away with their regiments. You shall see every one of them."

"Hurry, please, my time's limited!" the sergeant barked.

"I should think it would be—you're so

charming," Jane flung back over her shoulder, and she raised the tops of the baskets. The other women pushed forward with subdued coos.

The sergeant plunged his hand under a mass of colored fluffiness, groped for a minute, and brought forth a long roll of heavy paper. With a fierce mien, he began to unroll the bundle.

"And these?"

"Plans," Hildebrand's buyer answered.

"Plans of what?" The sergeant glared.

"Of gowns, silly! Here—you're looking at that one upside down! This way! Now isn't that a perfect dear of an afternoon gown? Poiret didn't have time to finish it, poor man! See that lovely basque effect? Everything's *moyen age* this season, you know."

Jane, with a shrewd sidelong glance at the flustered sergeant, rattled on, bringing gown after gown from the baskets and displaying them to the chorus of smothered screams of delight from the feminine part of her audience. One she draped coquettishly from her shoulders and did an exaggerated step before the smoky mirror over the mantelpiece to note the effect.

"Isn't it too bad this soldier person isn't married, so he could appreciate these beauties?" She flicked a mischievous eye his way. "Of course he can't be married, or he'd recognize the plan of a gown. Clean hands, there, Mister Sergeant, if you're going to touch any of these dreams! Here, let me! Now look at that *musquetaire* sleeve—the effect of the war —military, you know."

The sergeant was thoroughly angry by this time, and he forced the situation suddenly near tragedy. Under his fingers a delicate girdle crackled suspiciously.

"Here—your knife! Rip this open; there are papers of some sort hidden here." He started to pass the gown to one of his soldiers. Jane choked back a scream.

"No, no! That's crinoline, stupid! No papers——" She stretched forth her arms appealingly. The sergeant humped his shoulders and put out his hand to take the opened clasp-knife.

A plump doll-faced woman, who possessed an afterglow of prettiness and a bustling nervous manner, flounced through the doors at this juncture and burst suddenly into the midst of the group caught in the imminence of disaster.

"What's this—what's this?" She caught sight of the filmy creation draped from the sergeant's arm. "Oh, the beauty!" This in a whisper of admiration.

"The last one made by Worth," Jane was quick to explain, noting the sergeant's confusion in the presence of the stranger, "and this officer is going to rip it open in a search for concealed papers. He takes me for a spy."

Surprised blue eyes were turned from Jane to the sergeant. The latter shamefacedly tried to slip the open knife into his blouse, mumbling an excuse. The blue eyes bored him through.

"I call that very stupid, Sergeant," reproved the angel of rescue. Then to Jane——

"Where are you taking all these wonderful gowns?"

"To New York. I'm buyer for Hildebrand's, and——"

"But, Lady Crandall, this young woman has no passports—nothing," the sergeant interposed. "My duty——"

"Bother your duty! Don't you know a

Worth gown when you see it? Now go away! I'll be responsible for this young woman from now on. Tell your commanding officer Lady Crandall has taken your duty out of your hands." She finished with a quiet assurance and turned to gloat once more over the gowns. The sergeant led his command away with evident relief.

Lady Crandall turned to include all the refugees in a general introduction of herself.

"I am Lady Crandall, the wife of the governor general of Gibraltar," she said, with a warming smile. "I just came down to see what I could do for you poor stranded Americans. In these times——"

"An American yourself, I'll gamble on it!" Sherman pushed his way between the littered baskets and seized Lady Crandall's hands. "Knew it by the cut of your jib—and—your way of doing things. I'm Henry J. Sherman, from Kewanee, Illynoy—my wife and daughter Kitty."

"And I'm from Iowa—the red hills of ole Ioway," the governor's wife chanted, with an orator's flourish of the hands. "Welcome to the Rock, home folks!"

Hands all around and an impromptu old-home week right then and there. Lady Crandall's attention could not be long away from the gowns, however. She turned back to them eagerly. With Jane Gerson as her aid, she passed them in rapturous review, Mrs. Sherman and Kitty playing an enthusiastic chorus.

A pursy little man with an air of supreme importance—Henry Reynolds he was, United States Consul at Gibraltar—catapulted in from the street while the gown chatter was at its noisiest. He threw his hands above his head in a mock attitude of submissiveness before a highwayman.

" 'S all fixed, ladies and gentlemen," he cried, with a showman's eloquence. "Here's Lady Crandall come to tell you about it, and she's so busy riding her hobby—gowns and millinery and such—she has forgotten. I'll bet dollars to doughnuts."

"Credit to whom credit is due, Mister Consul," she rallied. "I'm not stealing anybody's official thunder." The consul wagged a forefinger at her reprovingly. With impatience, the refugees waited to hear the news.

"Well, it's this way," Reynolds began. "I've

got so tired having all you people sitting on
my door-step I just had to make arrangements
to ship you on the *Saxonia* in self-defense.
Saxonia's due here from Naples Thursday—
day after to-morrow; sails for New York at
dawn Friday morning. Lady Crandall, here
—and a better American never came out of
the Middle West—has agreed to go bond for
your passage money; all your letters of credit
and checks will be cashed by treasury agents
before you leave the dock at New York, and
you can settle with the steamship people right
there.

"No, no; don't thank me! There's the person responsible for your getting home." The
consul waved toward the governor's lady, who
blushed rosily under the tumultuous blessings
showered on her. Reynolds ducked out the
door to save his face. The Shermans made
their good nights, and with Kimball, started
toward the stairs.

"Thursday night, before you sail," Lady
Crandall called to them, "you all have an en-
gagement—a regular American dinner with
me at the Government House. Remember!"

"If you have hash—plain hash—and don't

call it a rag-owt, we'll eat you out of house and home," Sherman shouted as addendum to the others' thanks.

"And you, my dear"—Lady Crandall beamed upon Jane—"you're coming right home with me to wait for the *Saxonia's* sailing. Oh, no, don't be too ready with your thanks. This is pure selfishness on my part. I want you to help plan my fall clothes. There, the secret's out. But with all those beautiful gowns, sure- ly Hildebrand will not object if you leave the pattern of one of them in an out-of-the-way little place like this. Come on, now, I'll not take no for an answer. We'll pack up all these beauties and have you off in no time."

Jane's thanks were ignored by the capable packer who smoothed and straightened the confections of silk and satin in the osier ham- pers. Lady Crandall summoned the porter to lift the precious freight to the back of her dog- cart, waiting outside. Almer, perturbed at the kidnaping of his guest, came from behind the desk.

"You will go to your room now?" he queried anxiously.

"Not going to take it," Jane answered.

Lady Crandall beamed upon Jane.

"Have an invitation from Lady Crandall to visit the State House, or whatever you call it."

"But, pardon me. The room—it was rented, and I fear one night's lodging is due. Twenty shillings."

Jane elevated her eyebrows, but handed over a bill.

"Ah, no, lady. French paper—it is worthless to me. Only English gold, if the lady pleases." Almer's smile was leonine.

"But it's all I've got; just came from France, and——"

"Then, though it gives me the greatest sorrow, I must hold your luggage until you have the money changed. Excuse——"

Captain Woodhouse, who had dallied long over his dinner for lack of something else to do, came out of the dining-room just then, saw a woman in difficulties with the landlord, and instinctively stepped forward to offer his services.

"Beg pardon, but can I be of any help?"

Jane turned. The captain's heart gave a great leap and then went cold. Frank pleasure followed the first surprise in the girl's eyes.

"Why, Captain Woodhouse—how jolly!—To see you again after——."

She put out her hand with a free gesture of comradeship.

Captain Woodhouse did not see the girl's hand. He was looking into her eyes coldly, aloofly.

"I beg your pardon, but aren't you mistaken?"

"Mistaken?" The girl was staring at him, mystified.

"I'm afraid I have not had the pleasure of meeting you," he continued evenly. "But if I can be of service—now——"

She shrugged her shoulders and turned away from him.

"A small matter. I owe this man twenty shillings, and he will not accept French paper. It's all I have."

Woodhouse took the note from her.

"I'll take it gladly—perfectly good." He took some money from his pocket and looked at it. Then, to Almer: "I say, can you split a crown?"

"Change for you in a minute, sir—the tobacco shop down the street." Almer pocketed the gold piece and dodged out of the door.

Jane turned and found the deep-set gray eyes of Captain Woodhouse fixed upon her. They craved pardon—toleration of the incident just passed.

CHAPTER IX

ROOM D

WOODHOUSE hurried to Jane Gerson's side and began to speak swiftly and earnestly:

"You are from the States?"

A shrug was her answer. The girl's face was averted, and in the defiant set of her shoulders Woodhouse found little promise of pardon for the incident of the minute before. He persisted:

"This war means nothing to you—one side or the other?"

"I have equal pity for them both," she answered in a low voice.

"We are living in dangerous times," he continued earnestly. "I tell you frankly, were the fact that you and I had met before to become known here on the Rock the consequences would be most—inconvenient—for me." Jane turned

136

and looked searchingly into his face. Something in the tone rather than the words roused
her quick sympathy. Woodhouse kept on:

"I am sorry I had to deny that former meeting just now—that meeting which has been
with me in such vivid memory. I regret that
were you to allude to it again I would have to
deny it still more emphatically."

"I'm sure I shan't mention it again," the girl
broke in shortly.

"Perhaps since it means so little to you—
your silence—perhaps you will do me that
favor, Miss Gerson."

"Certainly." Woodhouse could see that
anger still tinged her speech.

"May I go further—and ask you to—promise?" A shadow of annoyance creased her
brow, but she nodded.

"That is very good of you," he thanked her.
"Shall you be long on the Rock?"

"No longer than I have to. I'm sailing on
the first boat for the States," she answered.

"Then I am in luck—to-night." Woodhouse
tried to speak easily, though Jane Gerson's attitude was distant. "Meeting you again—
that's luck."

"To judge by what you have just said it must be instead a great misfortune," she retorted, with a slow smile.

"That is not fair. You know what I mean. Don't imagine I've really forgotten our first meeting under happier conditions than these. I know I'm not clever—I can't make it sound as I would—but I've thought a great deal of you, Miss Gerson—wondering how you were making it in this great war. Perhaps——"

Almer returned at this juncture with the change, which he handed to Woodhouse. He was followed in by Lady Crandall, who assured Jane her hampers were securely strapped to the dog-cart. Jane attempted an introduction.

"This gentleman has just done me a service, Lady Crandall. May I present——"

"So sorry. You don't know my name. My clumsiness. Captain Woodhouse." The man bridged the dangerous gap hurriedly. Lady Crandall acknowledged the introduction with a gracious smile.

"Your husband is Sir George——" he began.

"Yes, Sir George Crandall, Governor-general of the Rock. And you——"

"Quite a recent comer. Transferred from the Nile country here. Report to-morrow."

"All of the new officers have to report to the governor's wife as well," Lady Crandall rallied, with a glance at Jane. "You must come and see me—and Miss Gerson, who will be with me until her boat sails."

Woodhouse caught his breath. Jane Gerson, who knew him, at the governor's home! But he mastered himself in a second and bowed his thanks. Lady Crandall was moving toward the door. Her ward turned and held out a hand to Woodhouse.

"So good of you to have straightened out my finances," she said, with a smile in which the man hoped he read full forgiveness for his denial of a few minutes before. "If you're ever in America I hope——" He looked up quickly. "I hope somebody will be as nice to you. Good night."

Woodhouse and Almer were alone in the mongrel reception room. The hour was late. Almer began sliding folding wooden shutters across the back of the street windows. Woodhouse lingered over the excuse of a final cigarette, knowing the moment for his rapprochement with his fellow Wilhelmstrasse spy was at hand. He was more distraught than he cared to admit even to himself. The day's developments had been startling. First the stunning encounter with Capper there on the very Rock that was to be the scene of his delicate operations—Capper, whom he had thought sunk in the oblivion of some Alexandrian wine shop, but who had followed him on the *Princess Mary*. The fellow had deliberately cast himself into his notice, Woodhouse reflected; there had been menace and insolent hint of a power to harm in his sneering objurgation that Woodhouse should remember his name against a second meeting. "Capper—never heard the name in Alexandria, eh?" What could he mean by that if not that somehow the little ferret had learned of his visit to the home of Doctor Koch? And that meant—why, Capper in Gibraltar was as dangerous as a coiled cobra!

Then the unexpected meeting with Jane Gerson, the little American he had mourned as lost in the fury of the war. Ah, that was a joy not unmixed with regrets! What did she think of him? First, he had been forced coldly to

deny the acquaintance that had meant much
to him in moments of recollection; then, he had
attempted a lame explanation, which explained
nothing and must have left her more mystified
than before. In fact, he had frankly thrown
himself on the mercy of a girl on whom he
had not the shadow of claim beyond the poor
equity of a chance friendship—an incident she
might consider as merely one of a day's travel
as far as he could know. He had stood before
her caught in a deceit, for on the occasion of
that never-to-be-forgotten ride from Calais to
Paris he had represented himself as hurrying
back to Egypt, and here she found him still
out of uniform and in a hotel in Gibraltar.

Beyond all this, Jane Gerson was going to
the governor's house as a guest. She, whom
he had forced, ever so cavalierly, into a promise to keep secret her half knowledge of the
double game he was playing, was going to be
on the intimate ground of associatiton with the
one man in Gibraltar who by a crook of his
finger could end suspicion by a firing squad.
This breezy little baggage from New York
carried his life balanced on the rosy tip of her
tongue. She could be careless or she could be

indifferent; in either case it would be bandaged eyes and the click of shells going home for him.

It was Almer who interrupted Woodhouse's troubled train of thought.

"Captain Woodhouse will report for signal duty on the Rock to-morrow, I suppose?" he insinuated, coming down to where Woodhouse was standing before the fireplace. He made a show of tidying up the scattered magazines and folders on the table.

"Report for signal duty?" the other echoed coldly. "How did you know I was to report for signal duty here?"

"In the press a few weeks ago," the hotel keeper hastily explained. "Your transfer from the Nile country was announced. We poor people here in Gibraltar, we have so little to think about, even such small details of news——"

"Ah, yes. Quite so." Woodhouse tapped back a yawn.

"Your journey here from your station on the Nile—it was without incident?" Almer eyed his guest closely. The latter permitted his eyes to rest on Almer's for a minute before replying.

"Quite." Woodhouse threw his cigarette in the fireplace and started for the stairs.

"Ah, most unusual—such a long journey without incident of any kind in this time of universal war, with all Europe gone mad." Almer was twiddling the combination of a small safe set in the wall by the fireplace, and his chatter seemed only incidental to the absorbing work he had at hand. "How will the madness end, Captain Woodhouse? What will be the boundary lines of Europe's nations in— say, 1932?"

Almer rose as he said this and turned to look squarely into the other's face. Woodhouse met his gaze steadily and without betraying the slightest emotion.

"In 1932—I wonder," he mused, and into his speech unconsciously appeared that throaty intonation of the Teutonic tongue.

"Don't go yet, Captain Woodhouse. Before you retire I want you to sample some of this brandy." He brought out of the safe a short squat bottle and glasses. "See, I keep it in the safe, so precious it is. Drink with me, Captain, to the monarch you have come to Gibraltar to serve—to his majesty, King George the Fifth!"

Almer lifted his glass, but Woodhouse appeared wrapped in thought; his hand did not go up.

"I see you do not drink to that toast, Captain."

"No—I was thinking—of 1932."

"So?" Quick as a flash Almer caught him up. "Then perhaps I had better say, drink to the greatest monarch in Europe."

"To the greatest monarch in Europe!" Woodhouse lifted his glass and drained it.

Almer leaned suddenly across the table and spoke tensely: "You have—something maybe —I would like to see. Some little relic of Alexandria, let us say."

Woodhouse swept a quick glance around, then reached for the pin in his tie.

"A scarab; that's all."

In the space of a breath Almer had seen what lay in the back of the stone beetle. He gripped Woodhouse's hand fervently.

"Yes—yes, Nineteen Thirty-two! They have

told me of your coming. A cablegram from
Koch only this afternoon said you would be on
the *Princess Mary*. The other—the real Woodhouse—there will be no slips; he will not——"

"He is as good as a dead man for many
months," Woodhouse interrupted. "Not a
chance of a mistake." He slipped easily into
German. "Everything depends on us now,
Herr Almer."

"Perhaps the fate of our fatherland," Almer
replied, cleaving to English. Woodhouse
stepped suddenly away from the side of the
table, against which he had been leaning, and
his right hand jerked back to a concealed holster on his hip. His eyes were hot with suspicion.

"You do not answer in German; why not?
Answer me in German or by——"

"*Ach!* What need to become excited?" Almer drew back hastily, and his tongue speedily
switched to German. "German is dangerous
here on the Rock, Captain. Only yesterday
they shot a man against a wall because he
spoke German too well. Do you wonder I try
to forget our native tongue?"

Woodhouse was mollified, and he smiled

apologetically. Almer forgave him out of admiration for his discretion.

"No need to suspect me—Almer. They will tell you in Berlin how for twenty years I have served the Wilhelmstrasse. But never before such an opportunity—such an opportunity. Stupendous!" Woodhouse nodded enthusiastic affirmation. "But to business, Nineteen Thirty-two. This Captain Woodhouse some seven years ago was stationed here on the Rock for just three months."

"So I know."

"You, as Woodhouse, will be expected to have some knowledge of the signal tower, to which you will have access." Almer climbed a chair on the opposite side of the room, threw open the face of the old Dutch clock there, and removed from its interior a thin roll of blue drafting paper. He put it in Woodhouse's hands. "Here are a few plans of the interior of the signal tower—the best I could get. You will study them to-night; but give me your word to burn them before you sleep."

"Very good." Woodhouse slipped the roll into the breast pocket of his coat. Almer leaned forward in a gust of excitement, and, bringing his mouth close to the other's ear, whispered hoarsely:

"England's Mediterranean fleet—twenty-two dreadnaughts, with cruisers and destroyers— nearly a half of Britain's navy, will be here any day, hurrying back to guard the Channel. They will anchor in the straits. Our big moment—it will be here then! Listen! Room D in the signal tower—that is the room. All the electric switches are there. From Room D every mine in the harbor can be exploded in ten seconds."

"Yes, but how to get to Room D?" Woodhouse queried.

"Simple. Two doors to Room D, Captain; an outer door like any other; an inner door of steel, protected by a combination lock like a vault's door. Two men on the Rock have that combination: Major Bishop, chief signal officer, he has in it his head; the governor-general of the Rock, he has it in his safe."

"We can get it out of the safe easier than from Major Bishop's head," Woodhouse put in, with a smile.

"Right. We have a friend—in the governor's own house—a man with a number from

the Wilhelmstrasse like you and me. At any
moment in the last two months he could have
laid a hand on that combination. But we
thought it better to wait until necessity came.
When the fleet arrives you will have that combination; you will go with it to Room D, and
after that——"

"The deluge," the other finished.

"Yes—yes! Our country master of the sea
at last, and by the work of the Wilhelmstrasse
—despised spies who are shot like dogs when
they're caught, but die heroes' deaths." The
hotel proprietor checked himself in the midst
of his rhapsody, and came back to more practical details:

"But this afternoon—that man from Alexandria who called you by name. That looked bad
—very bad. He knows something?"

Woodhouse, who had been expecting the
question, and who preferred not to share an
anxiety he felt himself best fitted to cope with
alone, turned the other's question aside:

"Never met him before in my life to my best
recollection. My name he picked up on the
Princess Mary, of course; I won a pool one
day, and he may have heard some one mention

it. Simply a drunken brawler who didn't know what he was doing."

Almer seemed satisfied, but raised another point:

"But the girl who has just left here; am I to have no explanation of her?"

"What explanation do you want?" the captain demanded curtly.

"She recognized you. Who is she? What is she?"

"Devilish unfortunate," Woodhouse admitted. "We met a few weeks ago on a train, while I was on my way to Egypt, you know. Chatted together—oh, very informally. She is a capable young woman from the States—a 'buyer' she calls herself. But I don't think we need fear complications from that score; she's bent only on getting home."

"The situation is dangerous," urged Almer, wagging his head. "She is stopping at the governor's house; any reference she might make about meeting you on a train on the Continent when you were supposed to be at Wady Halfa on the Nile——"

"I have her promise she will not mention that meeting to anybody."

"*Ach!* A woman's promise!" Almer's eyes invoked Heaven to witness a futile thing. "She seemed rather glad to see you again; I——"

"Really?" Woodhouse's eyes lighted.

The Splendide's proprietor was pacing the floor as fast as his fat legs would let him. "Something must be done," he muttered again and again. He halted abruptly before Woodhouse, and launched a thick forefinger at him like a torpedo.

"You must make love to that girl, Woodhouse, to keep her on our side," was his ultimatum.

Woodhouse regarded him quizzically, leaned forward, and whispered significantly.

"I'm already doing it," he said.

CHAPTER X

A VISIT TO A LADY

TURNING to consider the never-stale fortunes of one of fate's bean bags——

Mr. Billy Capper, ejected from the Hotel Splendide, took little umbrage at such treatment; it was not an uncommon experience, and, besides, a quiet triumph that would not be dampened by trifles filled his soul. Cheerfully he pushed through the motley crowd on Waterport Street down to the lower levels of the city by the Line Wall, where the roosts of sailors and warrens of quondam adventurers off all the seven seas made far more congenial atmosphere than that of the Splendide's hollow pretense. He chose a hostelry more commensurate with his slender purse than Almer's, though as a matter of fact the question of paying a hotel bill was furthest from Billy Capper's thoughts; such formal transactions he avoided whenever feasible. The proprietor of the San Roc, where Capper took a room, had such an evil eye that his new guest made a mental note that perhaps he might have to leave his bag behind when he decamped. Capper abhorred violence—to his own person.

Alone over a glass of thin wine—the champagne days, alas! had been too fleeting—Capper took stock of his situation and conned the developments he hoped to be the instrument for starting. To begin with, finances were wretchedly bad, and that was a circumstance so near the ordinary for Capper that he shuddered as he pulled a gold guinea and a few silver bits from his pocket, and mechanically counted them over. Of the three hundred marks Louisa—pretty snake!—had given him in the Café Riche and the expense money he had received from her the following day to cover his expedition to Alexandria for the Wilhelmstrasse naught but this paltry residue! That second-cabin ticket on the *Princess Mary* had taken the last big bite from his hoard, and here he was in this black-and-tan town with a quid and little more between himself and the old starved-dog life.

But—and Capper narrowed his eyes and

sagely wagged his head—there'd be something fat coming. When he got knee to knee with the governor-general of the Rock, and told him what he, Billy Capper, knew about the identity of Captain Woodhouse, newly transferred to the signal service at Gibraltar, why, if there wasn't a cool fifty pounds or a matter of that as honorarium from a generous government Billy Capper had missed his guess; that's all.

"I say, Governor, of course this is very handsome of you, but I didn't come to tell what I know for gold. I'm a loyal Englishman, and I've done what I have for the good of the old flag."

"Quite right, Mr. Capper; quite right. But you will please accept this little gift as an inadequate recognition of your loyalty. Your name shall be mentioned in my despatches home."

Capper rehearsed this hypothetical dialogue with relish. He could even catch the involuntary gasp of astonishment from the governor when that responsible officer in his majesty's service heard the words Capper would whisper to him; could see the commander of the Rock open a drawer in his desk and take therefrom

a thick white sheaf of bank-notes — count
them! Then—ah, then—the first train for
Paris and the delights of Paris at war-time
prices.

The little spy anticipated no difficulty in
gaining audience with the governor. Before
he had been fifteen minutes off the *Princess
Mary* he had heard the name of the present
incumbent of Government House. Crandall—
Sir George Crandall; the same who had been
in command of the forts at Rangoon back in
'99. Oh, yes, Capper knew him, and he made
no doubt that, if properly reminded of a certain bit of work Billy Capper had done back in
the Burmese city, Sir George would recall him
—and with every reason for gratefulness. To-
morrow—yes, before ever Sir George had had
his morning's peg, Capper would present himself at Government House and tell about that
house on Queen's Terrace at Ramleh; about
the unconscious British officer who was carried
there and hurried thence by night, and the
tall well-knit man in conference with Doctor
Koch who was now come to be a part of the
garrison of the Rock under the stolen name of
Woodhouse.

Capper had his dinner, then strolled around the town to see the sights and hear what he could hear. Listening was a passion with him.

For the color and the exotic savor of Gibral-- tar on a hot August night Capper had no eye. The knife edge of a moon slicing the battlements of the old Moorish Castle up on the heights; the minor tinkle of a guitar sounding from a vine-curtained balcony; a Riffian muleteer's singsong review of his fractious beast's degraded ancestry—not for these incidentals did the practical mind under the battered Capper bowler have room. Rather the scraps of information and gossip passed from one bluecoated artilleryman off duty, to another over a mug of ale, or the confidence of a sloe-eyed dancer to the guitar player in a tavern; this was meat for Capper. Carefully he husbanded his gold piece, and judiciously he spent his silver for drink. He enjoyed himself in the ascetic spirit of a monk in a fast, believing that the morrow would bring champagne in place of the thin wine his pitiful silver could command.

Then, of a sudden, he caught a glimpse of

Louisa—Louisa of the Wilhelmstrasse. Capper's heart skipped, and an involuntary impulse crooked his fingers into claws.

The girl was just coming out of a café—the only café aspiring to Parisian smartness Gibraltar boasts. Her head was bare. Under an arm she had tucked a stack of cigar boxes. Had it not been that a steady light from an overhead arc cut her features out of the soft shadow with the fineness of a diamond-pointed tool, Capper would have sworn his eyes were playing him tricks. But Louisa's features were unmistakable, whether in the Lucullian surroundings of a Berlin summer garden or here on a street in Gibraltar. Capper had instinctively crushed himself against the nearest wall on seeing the girl; the crowd had come between himself and her, and she had not seen him.

All the weasel instinct of the man came instantly to the fore that second of recognition, and the glint in his eyes and baring of his teeth were flashed from brute instinct—the instinct of the night-prowling meat hunter. All the vicious hate which the soul of Billy Capper could distil flooded to his eyes and made them venomous. Slinking, dodging, covering, he followed the girl with the cigar boxes. She entered several dance-halls, offered her wares at the door of a cheap hotel. For more than an hour Capper shadowed her through the twisting streets of the old Spanish town. Finally she turned into a narrow lane, climbed flagstone steps, set the width of the lane, to a house under the scarp of a cliff, and let herself in at the street door. Capper, following to the door as quickly as he dared, found it locked.

The little spy was choking with a lust to kill; his whole body trembled under the pulse of a murderous passion. He had found Louisa —the girl who had sold him out—and for her private ends, Capper made no doubt of that. Some day he had hoped to run her down, and with his fingers about her soft throat to tell her how dangerous it was to trick Billy Capper. But to have her flung across his path this way when anger was still at white heat in him— this was luck! He'd see this Louisa and have a little powwow with her even if he had to break his way into the house.

Capper felt the door-knob again; the door

wouldn't yield. He drew back a bit and looked up at the front of the house. Just a dingy black wall with three unlighted windows set in it irregularly. The roof projected over the gabled attic like the visor of a cap. Beyond the farther corner of the house were ten feet of garden space, and then the bold rock of the cliff springing upward. A low wall bounded the garden; over its top nodded the pale ghosts of moonflowers and oleanders.

Capper was over the wall in a bound, and crouching amid flower clusters, listening for possible alarm. None came, and he became bolder. Skirting a tiny arbor, he skulked to a position in the rear of the house; there a broad patch of illumination stretched across the garden, coming from two French windows on the lower floor. They stood half open; through the thin white stuff hanging behind them Capper could see vaguely the figure of a girl seated before a dressing mirror with her hands busy over two heavy ropes of hair. Nothing to do but step up on the little half balcony outside the windows, push through into the room, and—have a little powwow with Louisa.

An unwonted boldness had a grip on the lit-

tle spy. Never a person to force a face-to-
face issue when the trick could be turned
behind somebody's back, he was, nevertheless,
driven irresistibly by a furious anger that
took no heed of consequences.

With the light foot of a cat, Capper straddled the low rail of the balcony, pushed back
one of the partly opened windows, and stepped
into Louisa's room. His eyes registered mechanically the details—a heavy canopied bed,
a massive highboy of some dark wood, chairs
supporting carelessly flung bits of wearing ap-
parel. But he noted especially that just as he
emerged from behind one of the loose curtains
a white arm remained poised over a brown
head.

"Stop where you are, Billy Capper!" The
girl's low-spoken order was as cold and tense
as drawn wire. No trace of shock or surprise
was in her voice. She did not turn her head.
Capper was brought up short, as if he felt a
noose about his neck.

Slowly the figure seated before the dressing
mirror turned to face him. Tumbling hair
framed the girl's face, partly veiling the yellow-brown eyes, which seemed two spots of

metal coming to incandescence under heat.
Her hands, one still holding a comb, lay su-
pinely in her lap.

"I admit this is a surprise, Capper," Louisa
said, letting each word fall sharply, but without emphasis. "However, it is like you to be
—unconventional. May I ask what you want
this time—besides money, of course?"

Capper wet his lips and smiled wryly. He
had jumped so swiftly to impulse that he had
not prepared himself beforehand against the
moment when he should be face to face with
the girl from the Wilhelmstrasse. Moreover,
he had expected to be closer to her—very close
indeed—before the time for words should
come.

"I—I saw you to-night and followed you—
here," he began lamely.

"Flattering!" She laughed shortly.

"Oh, you needn't try to come it over me with
words!" Capper's teeth showed in a nasty
grin as his rage flared back from the first suppression of surprise. "I've come here to have
a settlement for a little affair between you and
me."

"Blackmail? Why, Billy Capper, how true

to form you run!" The yellow-brown eyes
were alight and burning now. "Have you determined the sum you want or are you in the
open market?"

Capper grinned again, and shifted his
weight, inadvertently advancing one foot a
little nearer the seated girl as he did so.

"Pretty quick with the tongue—as always,"
he sneered. "But this time it doesn't go, Louisa. You pay differently this time—pay for
selling me out. Understand!" Again one foot
shifted forward a few inches by the accident of
some slight body movement on the man's part.
Louisa still sat before her dressing mirror,
hands carelessly crossed on her lap.

"Selling you out?" she repeated evenly.
"Oh! So you finally did discover that you
were elected to be the goat? Brilliant Capper! How long before you made up your
mind you had a grievance?"

The girl's cool admission goaded the little
man's fury to frenzy. His mind craved for
action—for the leap and the tightening of fingers around that taunting throat; but somehow his body, strangely detached from the fiat
of volition as if it were another's body, lagged

to the command. Violence had never been its
mission; muscles were slow to accept this new
conception of the mind. But the man's feet
followed their crafty intelligence; by fractions
of inches they moved forward stealthily.

"You wouldn't be here now," Louisa coldly
went on, "if you weren't fortune's bright-eyed
boy. You were slated to be taken off the boat
at Malta and shot; the boat didn't stop at Malta through no fault of ours, and so you arrived
at Alexandria—and became a nuisance." One
of the girl's hands lifted from her lap and
lazily played along the edge of the rosewood
standard which supported the mirror on the
dressing table. It stopped at a curiously
carved rosette in the rococo scroll-work. Capper's suspicious eye noted the movement. He
sparred for time—the time needed by those
stealthy feet to shorten the distance between
themselves and the girl.

"Why," he hissed, "why did you give me a
number with the Wilhelmstrasse and send me
to Alexandria if I was to be caught and shot at
Malta? That's what I'm here to find out."

"Excellent Capper!" Her fingers were playing with the convolutions of the carved ros-

ette. "Intelligent Capper! He comes to a lady's room at night to find the answer to a simple question. He shall have it. He evidently does not know the method of the Wilhelmstrasse, which is to choose two men for every task to be accomplished. One—the 'target,' we call him—goes first; our friends whose secrets we seek are allowed to become suspicious of him—we even give them a hint to help them in their suspicion. They seize the 'target,' and in time of war he becomes a real target for a firing squad, as you should have been, Capper, at Malta. Then when our friends believe they have nipped our move in the bud follows the second man—who turns the trick."

Capper was still wrestling with that baffling stubbornness of the body. Each word the girl uttered was like vitriol on his writhing soul. His mind willed murder—willed it with all the strength of hate; but still the springs of his body were cramped—by what? Not cowardice, for he was beyond reckoning results. Certainly not compassion or any saving virtue of chivalry. Why did his eyes constantly stray to that white hand lifted to allow the fingers to play with the filigree of wood on the mirror support?

"Then you engineered the stealing of my number—from the hollow under the handle of my cane—some time between Paris and Alexandria?" he challenged in a whisper, his face thrust forward between hunched shoulders.

"No, indeed. It was necessary for you to have—the evidence of your profession when the English searched you at Malta. But the loss of your number is not news; Koch, in Alexandria, has reported, of course."

The girl saw Capper's foot steal forward again. He was not six feet from her now. His wiry body settled itself ever so slightly for a spring. Louisa rose from her chair, one hand still resting on the wooden rosette of the mirror standard. She began to speak in a voice drained of all emotion:

"You followed me here to-night, Billy Capper, imagining in your poor little soul that you were going to do something desperate—something really human and brutal. You came in my window all primed for murder. But your poor little soul all went to water the instant we faced each other. You couldn't nerve yourself to leap upon a woman even. You can't now."

She smiled on him—a woman's flaying smile of pity. Capper writhed, and his features twisted themselves in a paroxysm of hate.

"I have my finger on a bell button here, Capper. If I press it men will come in here and kill you without asking a question. Now you'd better go."

Capper's eyes jumped to focus on a round white nib under one of the girl's fingers there on the mirror's standard. The little ivory button was alive—a sentient thing suddenly allied against him. That inanimate object rather than Louisa's words sent fingers of cold fear to grip his heart. A little ivory button waiting there to trap him! He tried to cover his vanished resolution with bluster, sputtering out in a tense whisper:

"You're a devil—a devil from hell, Louisa! But I'll get you. They shoot women in war time! Sir George Crandall—I know him—I did a little service for him once in Rangoon. He'll hear of you and your Wilhelmstrasse tricks, and you'll have your pretty back

against a wall with guns at your heart before
to-morrow night. Remember—before to-morrow night!"

Capper was backing toward the open window behind him. The girl still stood by the
mirror, her hand lightly resting where the
ivory nib was. She laughed.

"Very well, Billy Capper. It will be a firing
party for two—you and me together. I'll
make a frank confession—tell all the information Billy Capper sold to me for three hundred
marks one night in the Café Riche—the story
of the Anglo-Belgian defense arrangements.
The same Billy Capper, I'll say, who sold the
Lord Fisher letters to the kaiser—a cable to
Downing Street will confirm that identification
inside of two hours. And then——"

"And your Captain Woodhouse—your cute
little Wilhelmstrasse captain," Capper flung
back from the window, pretending not to heed
the girl's potent threat; "I know all about him,
and the governor'll know, too—same time he
hears about you!"

"Good night, Billy Capper," Louisa answered, with a piquant smile. "And au

revoir until we meet with our backs against that wall."

Capper's head dropped from view over the balcony edge; there was a sound of running feet amid the close-ranked plants in the garden, then silence.

The girl from the Wilhelmstrasse, alone in the house save for the bent old housekeeper asleep in her attic, turned and laid her head— a bit weakly—against the carved standard, where in a florid rosette showed the ivory tip of the hinge for the cheval glass.

CHAPTER XI

A SPY IN THE SIGNAL TOWER

GOVERNMENT HOUSE, one of the Baedeker points of Gibraltar, stands amid its gardens on a shelf of the Rock about midway between the Alameda and the signal tower, perched on the very spine of the lion's back above it. Its windows look out on the blue bay and over to the red roofs of Algeciras across the water on Spanish territory. Tourists gather to peek from a respectful distance at the mossy front and quaint ecclesiastic gables of Government House, which has a distinction quite apart from its use as the home of the governor-general. Once, back in the dim ages of Spain's glory, it was a monastery, one of the oldest in the southern tip of the peninsula. When the English came their practical sense took no heed of the protesting ghosts of the monks, but converted the monastery into a

168

home for the military head of the fortress—
a little dreary, a shade more melancholy than
the accustomed manor hall at home, but ade-
quate and livable.

Thither, on the morning after his arrival,
Captain Woodhouse went to report for duty to
Major-general Sir George Crandall, Governor of
the Rock. Captain Woodhouse was in uniform
—neat service khaki and pith helmet, which
became him mightily. He appeared to have
been molded into the short-skirted, olive-gray
jacket; it set on his shoulders with snug ease.
Perhaps, if anything, the uniform gave to his
features a shade more than their wonted
sternness, to his body just the least addition
of an indefinable alertness, of nervous acute-
ness. It was nine o'clock, and Captain Woodhouse knew it was necessary for him to pay
his duty call on Sir George before the eleven
o'clock assembly.

As the captain emerged from the straggling
end of Waterport Street, and strode through
the flowered paths of the Alameda, he did not
happen to see a figure that dodged behind a
chevaux-de-frise of Spanish bayonet on his
approach. Billy Capper, who had been pacing

the gardens for more than an hour, fear battling with the predatory impulse that urged
him to Government House, watched Captain
Woodhouse pass, and his eyes narrowed into
a queer twinkle of oblique humor. So Captain
Woodhouse had begun to play the game—going
to report to the governor, eh? The pale soul
of Mr. Capper glowed with a faint flicker of
admiration for this cool bravery far beyond its
own capacity to practise. Capper waited a safe
time, then followed, chose a position outside
Government House from which he could see
the main entrance, and waited.

A tall thin East Indian with a narrow
ascetic face under his closely wound white tur-
ban, and wearing a native livery of the same
spotless white, answered the captain's summons
on the heavy knocker. He accepted the visitor's
card, showed him into a dim hallway hung
with faded arras and coats of chain mail. The
Indian, Jaimihr Khan, gave Captain Woodhouse a start when he returned to say the governor would receive him in his office. The
man had a tread like a cat's, absolutely noise-
less; he moved through the half light of the
hall like a white wraith. His English was

spoken precisely and with a curious mechanical intonation.

Jaimihr Khan threw back heavy double doors and announced, "Cap-tain Wood-house." He had the doors shut noiselessly almost before the visitor was through them.

A tall heavy-set man with graying hair and mustache rose from a broad desk at the right of a large room and advanced with hand outstretched in cordial welcome.

"Captain Woodhouse, of the signal service. Welcome to the Rock, Captain. Need you here. Glad you've come."

Woodhouse studied the face of his superior in a swift glance as he shook hands. A broad full face it was, kindly, intelligent, perhaps not so alert, as to the set of eyes and mouth as it had been in younger days when the stripes of service were still to be won. General Sir George Crandall gave the impression of a man content to rest on his honors, though scrupulously attentive to the routine of his position. He motioned the younger man to draw a chair up to the desk.

"In yesterday on the *Princess Mary*, I presume, Captain?"

"Yes, General. Didn't report to you on arrival because I thought it would be quite tea time and I didn't want to disturb——"

"Right!" General Crandall tipped back in his swivel chair and appraised his new officer with satisfaction. "Everything quiet on the upper Nile? Germans not tinkering with the Mullah yet to start insurrection or anything like that?"

"Right as a trivet, sir," Woodhouse answered promptly. "Of course we're anticipating some such move by the enemy—agents working in from Erythrea—holy war of a sort, perhaps, but I think our people have things well in hand."

"And at Wady Halfa, your former commander——" The general hesitated.

"Major Bronson-Webb, sir," Woodhouse was quick to supply, but not without a sharp glance at the older man.

"Yes—yes; Bronson-Webb — knew him in Rangoon in the late nineties—mighty decent chap and a good executive. He's standing the sun, I warrant."

Captain Woodhouse accepted the cigarette from the general's extended case.

"No complaint from him at least, General Crandall. We all get pretty well baked at Wady, I take it."

The governor laughed, and tapped a bell on his desk. Jaimihr Khan was instantly materialized between the double doors.

"My orderly, Jaimihr," General Crandall ordered, and the doors were shut once more. The general stretched a hand across the desk.

"Your papers, please, Captain. I'll receipt your order of transfer and you'll be a member of our garrison forthwith."

Captain Woodhouse brought a thin sheaf of folded papers from his breast pocket and passed it to his superior. He kept his eyes steadily on the general's face as he scanned them.

"C. G. Woodhouse—Chief Signal Officer— Ninth Grenadiers—Wady Halfa——" General Crandall conned the transfer aloud, running his eyes rapidly down the lines of the form. "Right. Now, Captain, when my orderly comes——"

A subaltern entered and saluted.

"This is Captain Woodhouse." General Crandall indicated Woodhouse, who had risen.

"Kindly conduct him to Major Bishop, who will assign him to quarters. Captain Woodhouse, we—Lady Crandall and I—will expect you at Government House soon to make your bow over the teacup. One of Lady Crandall's inflexible rules for new recruits, you know. Good day, sir."

Woodhouse, out in the free air again, drew in a long breath and braced back his shoulders. He accompanied the subaltern over the trails on the Rock to the quarters of Major Bishop, chief signal officer, under whom he was to be junior in command. But one regret marked his first visit to Government House— he had not caught even a glimpse of the little person calling herself Jane Gerson, buyer.

But he had missed by a narrow margin. Piloted by Lady Crandall, Jane had left the vaulted breakfast room for the larger and lighter library, which Sir George had converted to the purpose of an office. This room was a sort of holy of holies with Lady Crandall, to be invaded if the presiding genius could be caught napping or lulled to complaisance. This morning she had the important

necessity of unobstructed light—not a general
commodity about Government House—to urge
in defense of profanation. For her guest carried under her arm a sheaf of plans—by such
sterling architects of women's fancies as
Worth and Doeuillet, and the imp of envy
would not allow the governor's wife to have
peace until she had devoured every pattern.
She paused in mock horror at the threshold of
her husband's sanctum.

"But, George, dear, you should be out by
this time, you know," Lady Crandall expos-
tulated. "Miss Gerson and I have something
—oh, tremendously important to do here."
She made a sly gesture of concealing the bundle of stiff drawing paper she carried. General Crandall, who had risen at the arrival of
the two invaders, made a show at capturing
the plans his wife held behind her back. Jane
bubbled laughter at the spectacle of so exalted
a military lion at play. The general possessed
himself of the roll, drew a curled scroll from
it, and gravely studied it.

"Miss Gerson," he said with deliberation,
"this looks to me like a plan of Battery B. I

am surprised that you should violate the hospitality of Government House by doing spy work from its bedroom windows."

"Foolish! You've got that upside down for one thing," Lady Crandall chided. "And besides it's only a chart of what the lady of Government House hopes soon to wear if she can get the goods from Holbein's, on Regent Street."

"You see, General Crandall, I'm attacking Government House at its weakest point," Jane laughed. "Been here less than twelve hours, and already the most important member of the garrison has surrendered."

"The American sahib, Reynolds," chanted Jaimihr Khan from the double doors, and almost at once the breezy consul burst into the room. He saluted all three with an expansive gesture of the hands.

"Morning, Governor—morning, Lady Crandall, and same to you, Miss Gerson. Dear, dear; this is going to be a bad day for me, and it's just started." The little man was wound up like a sidewalk top, and he ran on without stopping:

"General Sherman might have got some real

force into his remarks about war if he'd had a job like mine. Miss Gerson—news! Heard from the *Saxonia*. Be in harbor some time to-morrow and leave at six sharp following morning." Jane clapped her hands. "I've wired for accommodations for all of you—just got the answer. Rotten accommodations, but —thank Heaven—I won't be able to hear what you say about me when you're at sea."

"Anything will do," Jane broke in. "I'm not particular. I want to sail—that's all."

The consul looked flustered.

"Um—that's what I came to see you about, General Crandall." He jerked his head around toward the governor with a birdlike pertness. "What are you going to do with this young lady, sir?" Jane waited the answer breathlessly.

"Why—um—really, as far as we're concerned," Sir George answered slowly, "we'd be glad to have her stop here indefinitely. Don't you agree, Helen?"

"Of course; but——"

"It's this way," the consul interrupted Lady Crandall. "I've arranged to get Miss Gerson aboard, provided, of course, you approve."

"You haven't got a cable through regarding her?" the general asked. "Her passports—lost —lot of red tape, of course."

"Not a line from Paris even," Reynolds answered. "Miss Gerson says the ambassador could vouch for her, and——"

"Indeed he could!" Jane started impulsively toward the general. "It was his wife arranged my motor for me and advanced me money."

General Crandall looked down into her eager face indulgently.

"You really are very anxious to sail, Miss Gerson?"

"General Crandall, I'm not very good at these please-spare-my-lover speeches," the girl began, her lips tremulous. "But it means a lot to me—to go; my job, my career. I've fought my way this far, and here I am—and there's the sea out there. If I can't step aboard the *Saxonia* Friday morning it—it will break my heart."

Gibraltar's master honed his chin thoughtfully for a minute.

"Um—I'm sure I don't want to break anybody's heart—not at my age, miss. I see no good reason why I should not let you go if nothing happens meanwhile to make me change my mind." He beamed good humor on her.

"Bless you, General," she cried. "Hildebrand's will mention you in its advertisements."

"Heaven forbid!" General Crandall cried in real perturbation.

Jane turned to Lady Crandall and took both her hands.

"Come to my room," she urged, with an air of mystery. "You know that Doeuillet evening gown—the one in blue? It's yours, Lady Crandall. I'd give another to the general if he'd wear it. Now one fitting and——"

Her voice was drowned by Lady Crandall's: "You dear!"

"Be at the dock at five A. M. Friday to see you and the others off, Miss Gerson," Reynolds called after her. "Must go now—morning crowd of busted citizens waiting at the consulate to be fed. Ta-ta!" Reynolds collided with Jaimihr Khan at the double doors.

"A young man who wishes to see you, General Sahib. He will give no name, but he says a promise you made to see him—by telephone an hour ago."

"Show Mr. Reynolds out, Jaimihr!" the general ordered. "Then you may bring the young man in."

Mr. Billy Capper, who had, in truth, telephoned to Government House and secured the privilege of an interview even before the arrival of Woodhouse to report, and had paced the paths of the Alameda since, blowing hot and cold on his resolutions, followed the soft-footed Indian into the presence of General Crandall. The little spy was near a state of nervous breakdown. Following the surprising and unexpected collapse of his plan to do a murder, he had spent a wakeful and brandy-punctuated night, his brain on the rack. His desire to play informer, heightened now a hundred-fold by the flaying tongue of Louisa, was almost balanced by his fears of resultant consequences. Cupidity, the old instinct for preying, drove him to impart to the governor-general of Gibraltar information which, he hoped, would be worth its weight in gold; Louisa's promise of a party *à deux* before a firing squad, which he knew in his heart she would be capable of arranging in a desperate moment, halted him. After screwing up his courage to the point of telephoning for an appointment, Capper had wallowed in fear. He dared not stay away from Government House then for fear of arousing suspicion; equally he dared not involve the girl from the Wilhelmstrasse lest he find himself tangled in his own mesh.

At the desperate moment of his introduction to General Crandall, Capper determined to play it safe and see how the chips fell. His heart quailed as he heard the doors shut behind him.

"Awfully good of you to see me," he babbled as he stood before the desk, turning his hat brim through his fingers like a prayer wheel.

General Crandall bade him be seated. "I haven't forgotten you did me a service in Burma," he added.

"Oh, yes—of course," Capper managed to answer. "But that was my job. I got paid for that."

"You're not with the Brussels secret-service people any longer, then?"

The question hit Capper hard. His fingers fluttered to his lips.

"No, General. They—er—let me go. Suppose you heard that—and a lot of other things about me.   That I was a rotter—that I drank——"

"What I heard was not altogether complimentary," the other answered judiciously. "I trust it was untrue."

Capper's embarrassment increased.

"Well, to tell the truth, General Crandall—ah—I did go to pieces for a time. I've been playing a pretty short string for the last two years. But"—he broke off his whine in a sudden accession of passion—"they can't keep me down much longer. I'm going to show 'em!"

General Crandall looked his surprise.

"General, I'm an Englishman. You know that. I may be down and out, and my old friends may not know me when we meet—but I'm English. And I'm loyal!" Capper was getting a grip on himself; he thought the patriotic line a safe one to play with the commander of a fortress.

"Yes—yes. I don't question that, I'm sure," the general grunted, and he began to riffle some papers on his desk petulantly.

Capper pressed home his point. "I just want you to keep that in mind, General, while I talk. Just remember I'm English—and loyal."

The governor nodded impatiently.

Capper leaned far over the desk, and began in an eager whisper:

"General, remember Cook—that chap in Rangoon—the polo player?" The other looked blank. "Haven't forgotten him, General? How he lived in Burma two years, mingling with the English, until one day somebody discovered his name was Koch and that he was a mighty unhealthy chap to have about the fortifications. Surely——"

"Yes, I remember him now. But what——"

"There was Hollister, too. You played billiards in your club with Hollister, I fancy. Thought him all right, too—until a couple of secret-service men walked into the club one day and clapped handcuffs on him. Remember that, General?"

The commander exclaimed snappishly that he could not see his visitor's drift.

"I'm just refreshing your memory, General," Capper hastened to reassure. "Just reminding you that there isn't much difference between a German and an Englishman, after all—if the German wants to play the Englishman and knows his book. He can fool a lot of us."

"Granted. But I don't see what all this has to do with——"

"Listen, General!" Capper was trembling in his eagerness. "I'm just in from Alexandria— came on the *Princess Mary*. There was an Englishman aboard, bound for Gib. Name was Captain Woodhouse, of the signal service."

"Quite right. What of that?" General Crandall looked up suspiciously.

"Have you seen Captain Woodhouse, General?"

"Not a half hour ago. He called to report."

"Seemed all right to you—this Woodhouse?" Capper eyed the other's face narrowly.

"Of course. Why not?"

"Remember Cook, General! Remember Hollister!" Capper warned.

General Crandall exploded irritably: "What the devil do you mean? What are you driving at, man?"

The little spy leaped to his feet in his excitement and thrust his weasel face far across the desk.

"What do I mean? I mean this chap who calls himself Woodhouse isn't Woodhouse at all. He's a German spy—from the Wilhelmstrasse

"He's a German spy."

—with a number from the Wilhelmstrasse!
He's on the Rock to do a spy's work!"

"Pshaw! Why did Brussels let you go?"
General Crandall tipped back in his seat and
cast an amused glance at the flushed face before him.

Capper shook his head doggedly. "I'm not
drunk, General Crandall. I'm so broke I
couldn't get drunk if I would. So help me, I'm
telling God's truth. I got it straight——"
Capper checked his tumult of words, and did
some rapid thinking. How much did he dare
reveal! "In Alexandria, General—got it there
—from the inside, sir. Koch is the head of the
Wilhelmstrasse crowd there—the same Cook
you knew in Rangoon; he engineered the trick.
The wildest dreams of the Wilhelmstrasse have
come true. They've got a man in your signal
tower, General—in your signal tower!"

General Crandall, in whom incredulity was
beginning to give way to the first faint glim-
merings of conviction as to the possibility of
truth in the informer's tale, rallied himself
nevertheless to combat an aspersion cast on
a British officer.

"Suppose the Germans have a spy in my

signal tower or anywhere here," he began argu-
mentatively. "Suppose they learn every nook
and corner of the Rock—have the caliber and
range of every gun in our defense; they
couldn't capture Gibraltar in a thousand
years."

"I don't know what they want," Capper returned, with the injured air of a man whose
worth fails of recognition. "I only came here
to warn you that your Captain Woodhouse is
taking orders from Berlin."

"Come—come, man! Give me some proof to
back up this cock-and-bull story," General
Crandall snapped. He had risen, and was
pacing nervously back and forth.

Capper was secretly elated at this sign that
his story had struck home. He stilled the fluttering of his hands by an effort, and tried to
bring his voice to the normal.

"Here it is, General—all I've got of the story.
The real Woodhouse comes down from somewhere up in the Nile—I don't know where—
and puts up for the night in Alexandria to wait
for the *Princess Mary*. No friends in the town,
you know; nowhere to visit. Three Wilhelmstrasse men in Alexandria, headed by that

clever devil Cook, or Koch, who calls himself a
doctor now. Somehow they get hold of the
real Woodhouse and do for him—what I don't
know—probably kill the poor devil.

"General, I saw with my own eyes an unconscious British officer being carried away from
Koch's house in Ramleh in an automobile—two
men with him." Capper fixed the governor
with a lean index finger dramatically. "And
I saw the man you just this morning received as
Captain Woodhouse leave Doctor Koch's house
five minutes after that poor devil—the real
Woodhouse—had been carried off. That's the
reason I took the same boat with him to Gibraltar, General Crandall—because I'm loyal
and it was my duty to warn you."

"Incredible!"

"One thing more, General." Capper was
sorely tempted, but for the minute his whole-
some fear of consequences curbed his tongue.
"Woodhouse isn't working alone on the Rock;
you can be sure of that. He's got friends to
help him turn whatever trick he's after—maybe in this very house. They're clever people,
you can mark that down on your slate!"

"Ridiculous!" The keeper of the Rock was

fighting not to believe now. "Why, I tell you
if they had a hundred of their spies inside the
lines—if they knew the Rock as well as I do
they could never take it."

Capper rose wearily, the air of a misunderstood man on him.

"Perhaps they aren't trying to capture it. I
know nothing about that. Well—I've done my
duty—as one Englishman to another. I hope
I've told you in time. I'll be going now."

General Crandall swung on him sharply.
"Where are you going?" he demanded.

Capper shrugged his shoulders hopelessly.
Now was the minute he'd been counting on—
the peeling of crackling notes from a fat bundle, the handsome words of appreciation.
Surely General Crandall was ripe.

"Well, General, frankly—I'm broke. Haven't
a shilling to bless myself with. I thought perhaps——" Capper shot a keen glance at the
older man's face, which was partly turned from
him. The general appeared to be pondering.
He turned abruptly on the spy.

"A few drinks and you might talk," he challenged.

Capper grinned deprecatively. "I don't

know, General—I might," he murmured. "I've
been away from the drink so long that——"

"Where do you want to go?" General Crandall cut him off. "Of course, you don't want to
stay here indefinitely."

"Well—if I had a bit of money—they tell me
everybody's broke in Paris. Millionaires—and
everybody, you know. You can get a room at
the Ritz for the asking. That would be heaven
for me—if I had something in my pocket."

"You want to go to Paris, eh?" General
Crandall stepped closer to Capper, and his eyes
narrowed in scorn.

"If it could be arranged, yes, General." Capper was spinning the brim of his bowler between nervous fingers. He did not dare meet
the other's glance.

"Demmit, Capper! You come here to blackmail me! I've met your kind before. I know
how to deal with your ilk."

"So help me, General, I came here to tell you
the truth. I want to go to Paris—or anywhere
away from here; I'll admit that. But that had
nothing to do with my coming all the way here
from Alexandria—spending my last guinea on
a steamer ticket—to warn you of your danger.

I'm an Englishman and—loyal!" Capper was pleading now. All hope of reward had sped and the vision of a cell with subsequent investigations into his own record appalled him. General Crandall sat down at his desk and began to write.

"I don't know—at any rate, I can't have you talking around here. You're going to Paris."

Capper dropped his hat. At a tap of the bell, Jaimihr Khan appeared at the doors, so suddenly that one might have said he was right behind them all the time. General Crandall directed that his orderly be summoned. When the subaltern appeared, the general handed him a sealed note.

"Orderly, turn this gentleman over to Sergeant Crosby at once," he commanded, "and give the sergeant this note." Then to Capper: "You will cross to Algeciras, where you will be put on a train for Madrid. You will have a ticket for Paris and twenty shillings for expense en route. You will be allowed to talk to no one alone before you leave Gibraltar, and under no circumstances will you be allowed to return—not while I am governor-general, at least."

Capper, his face alight with new-found joy, turned to pass out with the orderly. He paused at the doorway to frame a speech of thanks, but General Crandall's back was toward him. "Paris!" he sighed in rapture, and the doors closed behind him.

CHAPTER XII

"DO YOU know, my dear, Cynthia Maxwell is simply going to die with envy when she sees me in this!"

The plump little mistress of Government House, standing before a full-length mirror, in her boudoir, surveyed herself with intense satisfaction. Her arms and neck burst startlingly from the clinging sheath of the incomparable Doeuillet gown that was Jane Gerson's *douceur* for official protection; in the flood of morning light pouring through the mulljoned windows Lady Crandall seemed a pink and white—and somewhat florid—lily in oloom out of time. Hildebrand's buyer, on her knees and with deft fingers busy with the soft folds of the skirt, answered through a mouthful of pins:

"Poor Cynthia; my heart goes out to her."

"Oh, it needn't!" Lady Crandall answered,

192

with a tilting of her strictly Iowa style nose. "The Maxwell person has made me bleed more than once here on the Rock with the gowns a fond mama sends her from Paris. But, honestly, isn't this a bit low for a staid middle-aged person like myself? I'm afraid I'll have trouble getting my precious Doeuillet past the censor." Lady Crandall plumed herself with secret joy.

Jane looked up, puzzled.

"Oh, that's old Lady Porter—a perfect dragon," the general's wife rattled on. "Poor old dear; she thinks the Lord put her on the Rock for a purpose. Her own collars get higher and higher. I believe if she ever was presented at court she'd emulate the old Scotch lady who followed the law of décolleté, but preserved her self-respect by wearing a red flannel chest protector. You must meet her."

"I'm afraid I won't have time to get a look at your dragon," Jane returned, with a little laugh, all happiness. "Now that Sir George has promised me I can sail on the *Saxonia* Friday——"

"You really must——" The envious eyes of Lady Crandall fell on the pile of plans—

potent Delphic mysteries to charm the heart
of woman—that lay scattered about upon the
floor.

Jane sat back on her heels and surveyed the
melting folds of satin with an artist's eye.

"If you only knew—what it means to me to
get back with my baskets full of French beauties! Why, when I screwed up my courage
two months ago to go to old Hildebrand and
ask him to send me abroad as his buyer—I'd
been studying drawing and French at nights
for three years in preparation, you see—he
roared like the dear old lion he is and said I
was too young. But I cooed and pleaded, and
at last he said I could come—on trial, and
so——"

"He'll purr like a pussy-cat when you get
back," Lady Crandall put in, with a pat on the
brown head at her knees.

"Maybe. If I can slip into New York with
my little baskets while all the other buyers
are still over here, cabling tearfully for money
to get home or asking their firms to send a
warship to fetch them—why, I guess the pen-
nant's mine all right."

The eternal feminine, so strong in Iowa's

transplanted stock, prompted a mischievous
question:

"Then you won't be leaving somebody behind when you sail—somebody who seemed
awfully nice and—*foreigny* and all that? All
our American girls find the moonlight over on
this side infectious. Witness me—a 'finishing
trip' abroad after school days—and see where
I've finished—on a Rock!" Lady Crandall
bubbled laughter. A shrewd downward sweep
of her eye was just in time to catch a flush
mounting to Jane's cheeks.

"Well, a Mysterious Stranger has crossed
my path," Jane admitted. "He was very nice,
but mysterious."

"Oh!" A delighted gurgle from the oider
woman. "Tell me all about it—a secret for
these ancient walls to hear."

Jane was about to reply when second
thought checked her tongue. Before her
flashed that strange meeting with Captain
Woodhouse the night before—his denial of
their former meeting, followed by his curious
insistence on her keeping faith with him by
not revealing the fact of their acquaintance.
She had promised—why she had promised she

could no more divine than the reason for his asking; but a promise it was that she would not betray his confidence. More than once since that minute in the reception room of the Hotel Splendide Jane Gerson had reviewed the whole baffling circumstance in her mind and a growing resentment at this stranger's demand, as well as at her own compliance with it, was rising in her heart. Still, this Captain Woodhouse was "different," and —this Jane sensed without effort to analyze— the mystery which he threw about himself but served to set him apart from the common run of men. She evaded Lady Crandall's probing with a shrug of the shoulders.

"It's a secret which I myself do not know, Lady Crandall—and never will."

Back to the o'erweening lure of the gown the flitting fancy of the general's lady betook itself.

"You—don't think this is a shade too young for me, Miss Gerson?" Anxiety pleaded to be quashed.

"Nonsense!" Jane laughed.

"But I'm no chicken, my dear. If you

would look me up in our family Bible back in
Davenport you'd find——"

"People don't believe everything they read
in the Bible any more," Jane assured her.
"Your record and Jonah's would both be open
to doubt."

"You're very comforting," Lady Crandall
beamed. Her maid knocked and entered on
the lady's crisp: "Come!"

"The general wishes to see you, Lady Crandall, in the library."

"Tell the general I'm in the midst of trying
on——" Lady Crandall began, then thought
better of her excuse. She dropped the shim-
mering gown from her shoulders and slipped
into a kimono.

"Some stuffy plan for entertaining somebody or other, my dear"—this to Jane. "The
real burden of being governor-general of the
Rock falls on the general's wife. Just slip
into your bonnet, and when I'm back we'll take
that little stroll through the Alameda I've
promised you for this morning." She clutched
her kimono about her and whisked out of the
room.

General Crandall, just rid of the dubious pleasure of Billy Capper's company, was pacing the floor of the library office thoughtfully. He looked up with a smile at his wife's entrance.

"Helen, I want you to do something for me," he said.

"Certainly, dear." Lady Crandall was not an unpleasing picture of ripe beauty to look on, in the soft drape of her Japanese robe. Even in his worry, General Crandall found himself intrigued for the minute.

"There's a new chap in the signal service— just in from Egypt—name's Woodhouse. I wish you would invite him to tea, my dear."

"Of course; any day."

"This afternoon, if you please, Helen," the general followed.

His wife looked slightly puzzled.

"This afternoon? But, George, dear, isn't that—aren't you—ah—rushing this young man to have him up to Government House so soon after his arrival?" She suddenly remembered something that caused her to reverse herself. "Besides, I've asked him to dinner—the dinner I'm to give the Americans to-morrow night before they sail."

General Crandall looked his surprise.

"You didn't tell me that. I didn't know you had met him."

"Just happened to," Lady Crandall cut in hastily. "Met him at the Hotel Splendide last night when I brought Miss Gerson home with me."

"What was Woodhouse doing at the Splendide?" the general asked suspiciously.

"Why, spending the night, you foolish boy. Just off the *Princess Mary*, he was. I believe he did Miss Gerson some sort of a service —and I met him in that way—quite informally."

"Did Miss Gerson—a service—hum!"

"Oh, a trifling thing! It seemed she had only French money, and that cautious Almer fellow wouldn't accept it. Captain Woodhouse gave her English gold for it—to pay her bill. But why——"

"Has Miss Gerson seen him since?" General Crandall asked sharply.

"Why, George, dear, how could she? We

haven't been up from the breakfast table an hour."

"Woodhouse was here less than an hour ago to pay his duty call and report," he explained. "I thought perhaps he might have met our guest somewhere in the garden as he was coming or going."

"He did send her some lovely roses." Lady Crandall brightened at this, to her, patent inception of a romance; she doted on romances. "They were in Miss Gerson's room before she was down to breakfast."

"Roses, eh? And they met informally at the Splendide only last night." Suspicion was weighing the general's words. "Isn't that a bit sudden? I say, do you think Miss Gerson and this Captain Woodhouse had met somewhere before last night?"

"I hardly think so—she on her first trip to the Continent and he coming from Egypt. But——"

"No matter. I want him here to tea this afternoon." The general dismissed the subject and turned to his desk. His lady's curiosity would not be so lightly turned away.

"All these questions—aren't they rather ab-

surd? Is anything wrong?" She ran up to
him and laid her hands on his shoulders.

"Of course not, dear." He kissed her lightly on the brow. "Now run along and play
with that new gown Miss Gerson gave you. I
imagine that's the most important thing on
the Rock to-day."

Lady Crandall gave her soldier-husband a
peck on each cheek, and skipped back to her
room. When he was alone again, General
Crandall resumed his restless pacing. Resolution suddenly crystallized, and he stepped to
the desk telephone. He called a number.

"That you, Bishop? . . . General Crandall
speaking. . . . Bishop, you were here on the
Rock seven years ago? . . . Good! . . . Pretty
good memory for names and faces, eh? . . .
Right! . . . I want you to come to Government House for tea at five this afternoon. . . .
But run over for a little talk with me some
time earlier—an hour from now, say. Rather
important. . . . You'll be here. . . . Thank
you."

General Crandall sat at his desk and tried to
bring himself down to the routine crying from
accumulated papers there. But the canker

Billy Capper had implanted in his mind would not give him peace. Major-general Crandall was a man cast in the stolid British mold; years of army discipline and tradition of the service had given to his conservatism a hard grain. In common with most of those in high command, he held to the belief that nothing existed—nothing could txist—which was not down in the regulations of the war office, made and provided. For upward of twenty-five years he had played the hard game of the service—in Egypt, in Burma, on the broiling rocks of Aden, and here, at last, on the key to the Mediterranean. During all those years he had faithfully pursued his duty, had stowed away in his mind the wisdom disseminated in blue-bound books by that corporate paragon of knowledge at home, the war office. But never had he read in anything but fluffy fiction of a place or a thing called the Wilhelmstrasse, reputed by the scriveners to be the darkest closet and the most potent of all the secret chambers of diplomacy. The regulations made no mention of a Wilhelmstrasse, even though they provided the brand of pipe clay that should brighten men's pith helmets and stipulated to the ounce an emergency ration. Therefore, to the official military mind at least, the Wilhelmstrasse was non-existent.

But here comes a beach-comber, a miserable jackal from the back alleys of society, and warns the governor-general of the Rock that he has a man from the Wilhelmstrasse—a spy bent on some unfathomable mission—in his very forces on the Rock. He says that an agent of the enemy has dared masquerade as a British officer in order to gain admission inside the lines of Europe's most impregnable fortress, England's precious stronghold, there to do mischief!

General Crandall's tremendous responsibility would not permit him to ignore such a warning, coming even from so low a source. Yet the man found himself groping blindly in the dark before the dilemma presented; he had no foot rule of precept or experience to guide him.

His fruitless searching for a prop in emergency was broken by the appearance of Jane Gerson in the door opening from Lady Crandall's rooms to the right of the library. The girl was dressed for the out-of-doors; in her arms was a fragrant bunch of blood-red roses, spraying out from the top of a bronze bowl. The girl hesitated and drew back in confusion at seeing the room occupied; she seemed eager to escape undetected. But General Crandall smilingly checked her flight.

"I—I thought you would be out," Jane stammered, "and——"

"And the posies——" the general interrupted.

"Were for you to enjoy when you should come back." She smiled easily into the man's eyes. "They'll look so much prettier here than in my room."

"Very good of you, I'm sure." General Crandall stepped up to the rich cluster of buds and sniffed critically. Without looking at the girl, he continued: "It appears to me as though you had already made a conquest on the Rock. One doesn't pick these from the cliffs, you know."

"I should hardly call it a conquest," Jane answered, with a sprightly toss of her head.

"But a young man sent you these flowers. Come—confess!" The general's tone was

bantering, but his eyes did not leave the piquant face under the chic summer straw hat
that shaded it.

"Surely. One of your own men—Captain
Woodhouse, of the signal service." Jane was
rearranging the stems in the bowl, apparently
ready to accept what was on the surface of
the general's rallying.

"Woodhouse, eh? You've known him for
a long time, I take it."

"Since last night, General. And yet some
people say Englishmen are slow." She
laughed gaily and turned to face him. His
voice took on a subtle quality of polite insistence:

"Surely you met him somewhere before Gibraltar."

"How could I, when this is the first time
Captain Woodhouse has been out of Egypt for
years?"

"Who told you that?" The general was
quick to catch her up. The girl felt a swift
stab of fear. On the instant she realized that
here was somebody attempting to drive into
the mystery which she herself could not un-

derstand, but which she had pledged herself
to keep inviolate. Her voice fluttered in her
throat as she answered:

"Why, he did himself, General."

"He did, eh? Gave you a bit of his history
on first meeting. Confiding chap, what! But
you, Miss Gerson—you've been to Egypt, you
say?"

"No, General."

Jane was beginning to find this cross-exam-
ination distinctly painful. She felt that already her pledge, so glibly given at Captain
Woodhouse's insistence, was involving her in
a situation the significance of which might
prove menacing to herself—and one other.
She could sense the beginnings of a strain between herself and this genial elderly gentleman, her host.

"Do you know, Miss Gerson"—he was speaking soberly now—"I believe you and Captain
Woodhouse have met before."

"You're at liberty to think anything you like,
General—the truth or otherwise." Her answer,
though given smilingly, had a sting behind it.

"I'm not going to think much longer. I'm going to *know!*" He clapped his lips shut over the last word with a smack of authority.

"Are you really, General Crandall?" The girl's eyes hardened just perceptibly. He took a turn of the room and paused, facing her. The situation pleased him no more than it did his breezy guest, but he knew his duty and doggedly pursued it.

"Come—come, Miss Gerson! I believe you're straightforward and sincere or I wouldn't be wasting my time this way. I'll be the same with you. This is a time of war; you understand all that implies, I hope. A serious question concerning Captain Woodhouse's position here has arisen. If you have met him before—as I think you have—it will be to your advantage to tell me where and when. I am in command of the Rock, you know."

He finished with an odd tenseness of tone that conveyed assurance of his authority even more than did the sense of his words. His guest, her back to the table on which the roses rested and her hands bracing her by their tense grip on the table edge, sought his eyes boldly.

"General Crandall," she began, "my training

in Hildebrand's store hasn't made me much of
a diplomat. All this war and intrigue makes
me dizzy. But I know one thing: this isn't my
war, or my country's, and I'm going to follow
my country's example and keep out of it."

General Crandall shrugged his shoulders and
smiled at the girl's defiance.

"Maybe your country may not be able to do
that," he declared, with a touch of solemnity.
"I pray God it may. But I'm afraid your resolution will not hold, Miss Gerson."

"I'm going to try to make it, anyway," she
answered.

Gibraltar's commander, baffled thus by a
neutral—a neutral fair to look on, in the
bargain—tried another tack. He assumed the
fatherly air.

"Lady Crandall and I have tried to show you
we were friends—tried to help you get home,"
he began.

"You've been very good to me," Jane broke in
feelingly.

"What I say now is spoken as a friend, not
as governor of the Rock. If it is true that you
have met Woodhouse before—and our conversation here verifies my suspicion—that very

fact makes his word worthless and releases
you from any promise you may have made not
to reveal this and what you may know about
him. Also it should put you on your guard—
his motives in any attentions he may pay you
can not be above suspicion."

"I think that is a personal matter I am perfectly capable of handling." Jane's resentment
sent the flags to her cheeks.

General Crandall was quick to back-water:
"Yes, yes! Don't misunderstand me. What I
mean to say is——"

He was interrupted by his wife's voice calling for Jane from the near-by room. Anticipating her interruption, he hurried on:

"For the present, Miss Gerson, we'll drop
this matter. I said a few minutes ago I intended shortly to—*know*. I hope I won't have
to carry out that—threat."

Jane was withdrawing one of the buds from
the jar. At his last word, she dropped it with
a little gasp.

"Threat, General?"

"I hope not. Truly I hope not. But, young
woman——"

She stooped, picked up the flower, and was

setting it in his buttonhole before he could re-
monstrate.

"This one was for you, General," she said,
and the truce was sealed. That minute, Lady
Crandall was wafted into the room on the
breeze of her own staccato interruption.

"What's this—what's this! Flirting with
poor old George—pinning a rose on my revered
husband when my back's turned? Brazen miss.
I'm here to take you off to the gardens at once,
where you can find somebody younger—and not
near so dear—to captivate with your tricks.
At once, now!"

She had her arm through Jane's and was
marching her off. An exchange of glances between the governor and Hildebrand's young
diplomat of the dollar said that what had passed
between them was a confidence.

Jaimihr Khan announced Major Bishop to
the general a short time later. The major, a
rotund pink-faced man of forty, who had the
appearance of being ever tubbed and groomed
to the pink of parade perfection, saluted his
superior informally, accepted a cigarette and
crossed his plump legs in an easy chair near the
general's desk. General Crandall folded his

arms on his desk and went direct to his subject:

"Major, you were here on the Rock seven years ago, you say?"

"Here ten years, General. Regular rock scorpion—old-timer."

"Do you happen to recall this chap Woodhouse whom I sent to you to report for duty in the signal tower to-day? Has transfer papers from Wady Halfa."

"Haven't met him yet, though Captain Carson tells me he reported at my office a little more than an hour ago—see him after parade. Woodhouse—Woodhouse——" The major propped his chin on his fingers in thought.

"His papers—army record and all that—say he was here on the Rock for three months in the spring of nineteen-seven," General Crandall urged, to refresh the other's memory.

Major Bishop stroked his round cheeks, tugged at one ear, but found recollection difficult.

"When I see the chap—so many coming and going, you know. Three months—bless me! That's a thin slice out of ten years."

"Major, I'm going to take you into my confidence," the senior officer began; then he related the incident of Capper's visit and repeated the charge he had made. Bishop sat aghast at the word "spy."

"Woodhouse will be here to tea this afternoon," continued Crandall. "While you and I ask him a few leading questions, I'll have Jaimihr, my Indian, search his room in barracks. I trust Jaimihr implicitly, and he can do the job smoothly. Now, Bishop, what do you remember about nineteen-seven—something we can lead up to in conversation, you know?"

The younger man knuckled his brow for a minute, then looked up brightly.

"I say, General, Craigen was governor then. But—um—aren't you a bit—mild; this asking of a suspected spy to tea?"

"What can I do?" the other replied, somewhat testily. "I can't clap an officer of his majesty's army into prison on the mere say-so of a drunken outcast who has no proof to offer. I must go slowly, Major. Watch for a slip from this Woodhouse. One bad move on his part, and he starts on his way to face a firing squad."

Bishop had risen and was slowly pacing the room, his eyes on the walls, hung with many portraits in oils.

"Well, you can't help admiring the nerve of the chap," he muttered, half to himself. "Forcing his way on to the Rock—why, he might as well put his head in a cannon's mouth."

"I haven't time to admire," the general said shortly. "Thing to do is to act."

"Quite right. Nineteen-seven, eh? Um——" He paused before the portrait of a young woman in a Gainsborough hat and with a sparkling piquant face. "By George, General, why not try him on Lady Evelyn? There's a fair test for you, now!"

"You mean Craigen's wife?" The general looked up at the portrait quizzically. "Skeleton's bones, Bishop."

"Right; but no man who ever saw her could forget. I know I never can. Poor Craigen!"

"Good idea, though," the older man acquiesced. "We'll trip him on Lady Evelyn."

Jaimihr Khan appeared at the double doors. "The general sahib's orderly," he announced. The young subaltern entered and saluted.

"That young man, General Crandall, the one Sergeant Crosby was to escort out of the lines to Algeciras——"

"Well, what of him? He's gone, I hope."

"First train to Madrid, General; but he left a message for you, sir, to be delivered after he'd gone, he said."

"A message?" General Crandall was perplexed.

"As Sergeant Crosby had it and gave it to me to repeat to you, sir, it was, 'Arrest the cigar girl calling herself Josepha. She is one of the cleverest spies of the Wilhelmstrasse.'"

CHAPTER XIII

MR. JOSEPH ALMER, proprietor of the Hotel Splendide, on Waterport Street, was absorbed, heart and soul, in a curious task. He was emptying the powder from two-grain quinine capsules on to a sheet of white letter paper on his desk.

It was noon of Wednesday, the day following the arrival of Captain Woodhouse. Almer was alone in the hotel's reception room and office behind the dingy glass partially enclosing his desk. His alpaca-covered shoulders were close to his ears; and his bald head, with its stripes of plastered hair running like thick lines of latitude on a polished globe, was held far forward so as to bring his eyes on the work in hand. Like some plump magpie he appeared, turning over bits of china in a treasure hole.

A round box of the gelatine cocoons lay at his left hand; it had just been delivered by an

Arab boy, quick to pick up the street commission for a tuppence. Very methodically Almer picked the capsules from the box one by one, opened them, and spilled the quinine in a little heap under his nose. He grunted peevishly when the sixth shell had been emptied. The seventh capsule brought an eager whistle to his lips. When he had jerked the concentric halves apart, very little powder fell out. Instead, the thin, folded edges of a pellet of rice paper protruded from one of the containers. This Almer had extracted in an instant. He spread it against the black back of a ledger and read the very fine script written thereon. This was the message:

"Danger. An informer from Alexandria has denounced our two friends to Crandall. You must warn; I can not."

The spy's heart was suddenly drained, and the wisp of paper in his hand trembled so that it scattered the quinine about in a thin cloud. Once more he read the note, then held a match to it and scuffed its feathery ash with his feet into the rug beneath his stool. The fortitude which had held Joseph Almer to the Rock in the never-failing hope that some day would bring him the opportunity to do a great service for the fatherland came near crumbling that minute. He groaned.

"Our friends," he whispered, "Woodhouse and Louisa—trapped!"

The warning in the note left nothing open to ambiguity for Almer; there were but four of them — "friends" under the Wilhelmstrasse fellowship of danger—there in Gibraltar: Louisa, the man who passed as Woodhouse, and whose hand was to execute the great coup when the right moment came, himself, and that other one whose place was in Government House itself. From this latter the note of warning had come. How desperate the necessity for it Almer could guess when he took into reckoning the dangers that beset any attempt at communication on the writer's part. So narrow the margin of safety for this "friend" that he must look at each setting sun as being reasonably the last for him.

Almer did not attempt to go behind the note and guess who was the informer that had lodged information with the governor-general.

He had forgotten, in fact, the incident of the
night before, when the blustering Capper called
the newly arrived Woodhouse by name. The
flash of suspicion that attached responsibility
to the American girl named Gerson was dis-
sipated as quickly as it came; she had arrived
by motor from Paris, not on the boat from
Alexandria. His was now the imperative duty
to carry warning to the two suspected, not to
waste time in idle speculation as to the identity
of the betrayer. There was but one ray of
hope in this sudden pall of gloom, and that
Almer grasped eagerly. He knew the character of General Crandall—the phlegmatic conservatism of the man, which would not easily
be jarred out of an accustomed line of thought
and action. The general would be slow to leap
at an accusation brought against one wearing
the stripes of service; and, though he might
reasonably attempt to test Captain Woodhouse,
one such as Woodhouse, chosen by the Wilhelmstrasse to accomplish so great a mission, would
surely have the wit to parry suspicion.

Yes, he must be put on his guard. As for
Louisa—well, it would be too bad if the girl
should have to put her back against a wall;

but she could be spared; she was not essential. After he had succeeded in getting word of his danger to Woodhouse, Almer would consider saving Louisa from a firing squad. The nimble mind of Herr Almer shook itself free from the incubus of dread and leaped to the exigency of the moment. Calling his head waiter to keep warm the chair behind the desk, Almer retired to his room, and there was exceedingly busy for half an hour.

The hour of parade during war time on Gibraltar was one o'clock. At that time, six days a week, the half of the garrison not actually in fighting position behind the great guns of the defense marched to the parade grounds down by the race track and there went through the grilling regimen that meant perfection and the maintenance of a hair-trigger state of efficiency. Down from the rocky eminences where the barracks stood, marched this day block after block of olive-drab fighting units—artillerymen for the most part, equipped with the rifle and pack of infantrymen. No blare of brass music gave the measure to their step; bandsmen in this time of reality paced two by two, stretchers carried between them. All the curl and snap

of silken banners that made the parade a
moving spectacle in ordinary times was absent;
flags do not figure in the grim modern business
of warfare. Just those solid blocks of men
trained to kill, sweeping down on to the level
grounds and massing, rank on rank, for in-
spection and the trip-hammer pound-pound-
pound of evolutions to follow. Silent integers
of power, flexing their muscles for the supreme
test that any morning's sun might bring.

Mr. Henry J. Sherman stood with his wife,
Kitty and Willy Kimball — Kimball had de-
veloped a surprising interest in one of these
home folks, at least—under the shade of the
row of plane trees fringing the parade grounds.
They tried to persuade themselves that they
were seeing something worth while. This
pleasing fiction wore thin with Mr. Sherman
before fifteen minutes had passed.

"Shucks, mother! The boys at the national-
guard encampment down to Galesburg fair last
year made a better showing than this." He
pursed out his lips and regarded a passing bat-
talion with a critical eye.

"Looked more like soldiers, anyway," mother
admitted. "Those floppy, broad-brimmed hats

our boys wear make them look more—more
romantic, I'd say."

"But, my dear Mrs. Sherman"—Willy Kimball flicked his handkerchief from his cuff and
fluttered it across his coat sleeve, where dust
had fallen—"the guards back in the States are
play soldiers, you know; these chaps, here—
well, they are the real thing. They don't dress
up like picture-book soldiers and show off——"

"Play soldiers—huh!" Henry J. had fire in
his eye, and the pearl buttons on his white linen
waistcoat creaked with the swelling of a
patriot's pride. "You've been a long time from
home, Willy. Perhaps you've forgotten that
your own father was at Corinth. Guess you've
overlooked that soldiers' monument in Court-
house Square back in little old Kewanee. They
were 'play soldiers,' eh?—those boys who
marched away with your dad in sixty-one.
Gimme a regiment of those old boys in blue, and
they could lick this whole bunch of——"

"Father!" Kitty had flipped her hand over
her parent's mouth, her eyes round with real
fear. "You'll get arrested again, talking that
way here where everybody can hear you. Remember what that hotel man said last night

about careless remarks about military things
on the Rock? Be good, father."

"There, there!" Sherman removed the mon-
itory hand and patted it reassuringly. "I forgot. But when I get aboard the *Saxonia* and
well out to sea, I'm going to just *bust* information about what I think of things in general
over here in this Europe place—their Botty-
celly pictures and their broken-down churches
and—and—— Why, bless my soul! The little
store buyer and that Iowa girl who's married
to the governor here!"

The patriot stopped short in his review of the
Continent's delinquencies to wave his hat at
Lady Crandall and Jane Gerson, who were
trundling down under the avenue of planes in
a smart dog-cart. Lady Crandall answered his
hail with a flourish of her whip, turned her
horse off the road, and brought her conveyance
to a stop by the group of exiles. Hearty greetings passed around. The governor's wife
showed her unaffected pleasure at the meeting.

"I thought you wouldn't miss the parade,"
she called down from her high seat. "Only
thing that moves on the Rock—these daily re-
views. Brought Miss Gerson down here so

when she gets back to New York she can say
she's seen the defenders of Gibraltar, if not in
action, at least doing their hard training for
it."

"Well, I don't mind tellin' you," Sherman began defiantly, "I think the national guard of
Illynoy can run circles around these Englishmen when it comes to puttin' up a show. Now,
Kitty, don't you try to drive a plug in your
dad's sentiments again; Mrs. Crandall's all
right—one of us." A shocked look from his
daughter. "Oh, there I go again, forgettin'.
Lady Crandall, I mean. Excuse me, ma'am."

"Don't you dare apologize," the governor's
wife playfully threatened Mr. Sherman with
her whip. "I love the sound of good, old-fash-
ioned 'Missis.' Just imagine—married five
years, and nobody has called me 'Mrs. Crandall'
until you did just now. 'Wedded, But Not a
Missis'; wouldn't that be a perfectly gorgeous
title for a Laura Jean novel? Miss Gerson, let's
hop out and join these home folks; they're my
kind."

The burst of laughter that greeted Lady
Crandall's sally was not over before she had
leaped nimbly from her high perch, Henry J.

gallantly assisting. Jane followed, and the
coachman from his little bob seat in the back
drove the dog-cart over the road to wait his
mistress' pleasure. The scattered blocks of
olive-gray on the field had coalesced into a solid
regiment now, and the long double rank of
men was sweeping forward like the cutting arm
of a giant mower. The party of Americans
joined the sparse crowd of spectators at the
edge of the field, the better to see. Jane Gerson found herself chatting with Willy Kimball
and Kitty Sherman a little apart from the
others. A light touch fell on her elbow. She
turned to find Almer, the hotel keeper, smiling
deferentially.

"Pardon—a thousand pardons for the intru-
sion, lady. I am Almer, of the Hotel Splendide."

"You haven't remembered something more I
owe you," Jane challenged bruskly.

"Oh, no, lady!" Almer spread out his hands.
"I happened to see you here watching the parade, and I remembered a trivial duty I have
which, if I may be so bold as to ask, you may
discharge much more quickly than I—if you
will."

"I discharge a duty—for you?" The girl did not conceal her puzzlement. Almer's hand fumbled in a pocket of his flapping alpaca coat and produced a plain silver cigarette case, unmonogrammed. She looked at it wonderingly.

"Captain Woodhouse—you met him at my hotel last night, lady. He left this lying on his dresser when he quit his room to go to barracks to-day. For me it is difficult to send a messenger with it to the barracks—war time, lady—many restrictions inside the lines. I came here hoping perhaps to see the captain after the parade. But you——"

"You wish me to give this to Captain Woodhouse?" Jane finished, a flicker of annoyance crossing her face. "Why me?"

"You are at Government House, lady. Captain Woodhouse comes to tea—all newcomers to the garrison do that. If you would be so good——"

Jane took the cigarette case from Almer's outstretched hand. Lady Crandall had told her the captain would be in for tea that afternoon. It was a small matter, this accommodation, as long as Almer did not insinuate—as he had not

done—any impertinence; imply any over eagerness on her part to perform so minor a service
for the officer.   Almer bowed his thanks and
lost himself in the crowd.   Jane turned again
to where Kitty and Kimball were chatting.

"A dun for extra service the landlord forgot
last night, I'll wager," the youth greeted her.

"Oh, no, just a little present," Jane laughed
back at him, holding up the silver case.   "With
Almer's compliments to Captain Woodhouse,
who forgot it when he gave up his room to-day.
I've promised to turn it over to the captain and
save the hotel man a lot of trouble and red tape
getting a messenger through to the captain's
quarters."

"By Jove!"   Kimball's tired eyes lighted up
with a quick flash of smoker's yearning.   "A
life-saver!   Came away from my room without
my pet Egyptians—Mr. Sherman yelling at me
to hurry or we'd miss this slow show and all
that.   I'm going to play the panhandler and beg
one of your captain friend's smokes.   He must
be a good sort or you wouldn't be doing little
favors for him, Miss Gerson.   Come, now; in
your capacity as temporary executrix will you

invest one of the captain's cigarettes in a demand of real charity?"

Keen desire was scarcely veiled under Kimball's fiction of light patter. Smilingly the girl extended the case to him.

"Just to make it businesslike, the executrix demands your note for—um—sixty days, say. 'For one cigarette received, I promise to pay——'"

"Given!" He pulled a gold pencil from his pocket and made a pretense of writing the form on his cuff. Then he lit his borrowed cigarette and inhaled it gratefully.

"Your captain friend's straight from Egypt; I don't have to be told that," Willy Kimball murmured, in polite ecstasy. "At Shepard's, in Cairo, you'll get such a cigarette as this, and nowhere else in a barren world. The breath of the acanthus blossom—if it really has a breath—never heard."

"Back in Kewanee the Ladies' Aid Society will have you arrested," Kitty put in mischievously. "They're terribly wrought up over cigarettes—for minors."

Kimball cast her a glance of deep reproach.

As he lifted the cigarette to his lips for a second puff, Jane's eyes mechanically followed the movement. Something caught and held them, wonder-filled.

On the side of the white paper cylinder nearest her a curious brown streak appeared—by the merest freak of chance her glance fell on it. As she looked, the thin stain grew darker nearest the fresh ash. The farther end of the faint tracing moved—yes, moved, like a threadworm groping its way along a stick.

"Now what are they all doing out there?" Kitty Sherman was asking. "All those men running top speed with their guns carried up so high."

"Bayonet charge," Kimball answered. "Nothing like the real thing, of course."

Jane Gerson was watching the twisting and writhing of that filament of brown against the white. An invisible hand was writing in brown ink on the side of the cigarette—writing backward and away from the burning tip. It lengthened by seconds—"and Louisa to Crandall."

So the letters of silver nitrate formed themselves under her eyes. Kimball took the ciga-

rette from his lips and held it by his side for
a minute. He and Kitty were busy with each
other's company for the time, ignoring Jane.
She burned with curiosity and with excitement
mounting like the fire of wine to her brain.
Would he never put that cigarette to his lips
again, so she could follow the invisible pen!
So fleeting, so evanescent that worm track
on the paper, wrought by fire and by
fire to be consumed. A mystery vanishing
even as it was aborning! After ages, the unconscious Kimball set the cigarette again in
his lips.

"—nformer has denounced you and Louisa-t-
—play your game and he will be slow to———"

Again the cigarette came away in Kimball's
hand. Acting on impulse she did not stop to
question, Jane struck it from the young man's
outstretched hand and set her foot on it as it
fell in the dust.

"Oh, I'm clumsy!" She fell lightly against
Kimball's shoulder and caught herself in well-
simulated confusion. "Standing tiptoe to see
what that man on a horse is going to do—lost

my balance. And—and your precious cigarette
—gone!"

The anguish in Jane Gerson's voice was not
play. It was real—terribly real.

CHAPTER XIV

THE CAPTAIN COMES TO TEA

JANE GERSON, alone for the first time
since the incident of the cigarette on the
parade ground a few hours back, sat before a
narrow window in her room at Government
House, fighting a great bewilderment. The
window opened on a varied prospect of bloom-
ing gardens and sail-flecked bay beyond. But
for her eyes the riot of color and clash of contrast between bald cliff and massed green had
no appeal. Her hands locked and unlocked
themselves on her lap. The girl's mind was
struggling to coordinate scattered circumstances into a comprehensible whole, to grapple
with the ethical problem of her own conduct.

What she knew, or thought she knew—and
what she should do—those were the two saber
points of the dilemma upon which she found
herself impaled.

Could there now be any doubt of what she
felt to be the truth? First, she had met Cap-

tain Woodhouse on the Express du Nord—an
officer in the English army, by his own state-
ment, returning from leave in England to his
post in Egypt. Then, the encounter of last
night at the Hotel Splendide, Captain Woodhouse first denying his identity, then admitting
it under the enforced pledge that she should
not reveal the former meeting. Captain Woodhouse, not in Egypt, but at Gibraltar, and, as
she had soon learned, there with papers of
transfer from an Egyptian post to the garrison
of the Rock. Following this surprise had come
General Crandall's dogged examination of that
morning—his blunt declaration that a serious
question as to the captain's position at Gibraltar had arisen, and his equally plain-spoken
threat to have the truth from her concerning
her knowledge of the suspected officer.

To cap all, the message on the cigarette! An
informer—she guessed the prefix to the unfin-
ished word—had denounced "you and Louisa"
to General Crandall. To whom the pronoun
referred was unmistakable—Almer's eagerness
to insure Captain Woodhouse's receiving the
cigarette case plainly defined that. As to
"Louisa," involved with Woodhouse, the girl

from Hildebrand's was sensible only of a passing flash of curiosity, made a bit more piquant,
perhaps, by a little dart of jealousy, hardly
comprehended as such. A hotel keeper warns
an officer in the Gibraltar garrison that he has
been denounced, but in the same message ad-
jures him to "play your own game." That was
the single compelling fact.

Jane Gerson flushed—in anger, or was it
through guilt?—when she found her lips fram-
ing the word "spy"!

Now she understood why General Crandall
had put her on the grill—why he, informed,
had leaped to the significance of the gift of
roses and deduced her previous acquaintance
with their donor. Her host was not, after all,
the possessor of magical powers of mind reading. He was, instead, just the sober, conscien-
tious protector of the Rock on whom rested
responsibility for the lives of its defenders and
the maintenance of England's flag there. His
duty was to catch—and shoot—spies.

Shoot spies! The girl's heart contracted at
the thought. No, no! She would not—she
could not reveal to the governor the knowledge
she had. That would be to send death to a

man as surely as if hers was the finger at the
trigger.

Jane Gerson was on her feet now, pacing
the room. Over and over again she told herself
that this man who had come into her life, ob-
liquely enough, had no claim on her; had
brought nothing to her but distress. He had
deceived her even, and then, when caught in
the deception, had wrested from her a promise
that she would help him continue further deception against others. Against her will he
had made her a party to some deep and auda-
cious plot, whose purpose she could not guess,
but which must be but a part of the huge mystery of war.

And soon this Captain Woodhouse was to
come to his trial—the purpose of his invitation to tea that afternoon flashed clear as white
light. Soon she would be in the same room
with him; would be forced to witness the spinning of the web set to trap him. He would
come unwarned, unsuspecting. He might leave
that room under guard and with guns at his
back—guns soon to be leveled at his heart. Yet
she, Jane Gerson, possessed the power to save
him—as the warning of the cigarette surely

would be saving, once a clever man were put on his guard by it.

Would she speak—and betray General Crandall, her kindly host? Would she lock her lips and see a man walk blindfolded to his death?

A few minutes before five o'clock, Major Bishop was announced at Government House and received by General Crandall in the library. Before Jaimihr Khan, who had preceded the visitor through the double doors from the hall, could retire, his master stopped him.

"One minute, Jaimihr! Have a seat, Bishop; glad you've come a bit early. Come here, Jaimihr!"

The tall reedlike figure of the Indian glided to General Crandall's side. His thin ascetic features were set in their usual mold of unseeing detachment; only his dark eyes showed animation.

"Yes, my General," he said, as he stopped before the Englishman.

"I have a little commission for you, Jaimihr," General Crandall began, weighing his words with care. "The utmost discretion—you understand?"

"The utmost. I understand." Jaimihr Khan's lips moved ever so slightly, and his eyes looked steadily ahead.

"In the course of a few minutes, Captain Woodhouse, of the signal service, will be here to tea," the general began. The Indian repeated mechanically: "Cap-tain Wood-house."

"As soon as you have ushered him into this room, you will go as quickly as you can to the West Barracks. His room will be No. 36, on the second gallery. You will enter his room with a, key I shall give you and search it from end to end—everything in it. Anything that is of a suspicious nature—you understand, Jaimihr, what that might be—you will bring here to me at once."

"It shall be done, General Sahib."

"No one, officer or man, must suspect your errand. No one must see you enter or leave that room."

"No one," the Indian repeated.

General Crandall went to a wall safe set by the side of the double doors, turned the combination, and opened it. He took from a drawer therein a bunch of keys, selected one, and passed it to Jaimihr Khan.

"The utmost care, remember!" he warned again.

"Is it likely I should fail you this time, General Sahib, when so many times I have succeeded?"

"Make the search complete." General Crandall ignored his servant's question. "But return as quickly as you can. I shall keep Captain Woodhouse here until you do so. You must report to me before he leaves this house."

"When the moment arrives, your servant shall fly, General Sahib," the Indian replied, and withdrew.

"I say, General, you have a great deal of faith in your Indian," Bishop ventured, accepting a cigarette from his superior's case. "Rather a delicate commission you've given him."

"Absolute faith, yes. Been with me five years—picked him up in Rangoon—have tried him many times, and found him loyal as any officer in the service." General Crandall put in his words enough emphasis to carry slight rebuke for the other's implied criticism. But the pursy little major was too sure of the fine terms of personal friendship between himself and his superior to feel embarrassment.

"About that girl, General—that cigar girl, Josepha, concerning whom your beach-comber friend sent that warning this morning from the safe ground of Spain——"

"Obvious thing would have been to clap her in a cell," the governor answered. "But I have not, for the very good reason that if there's anything in this fellow's accusations against her, as well as against Woodhouse, the game will be to keep her watched and give our captain an opportunity to communicate with her. Minute he does that—why, we've got our proof against both."

"Then I take it you've put a trailer on the girl?"

"At eight o'clock to-night I'll know where she's been every hour of the day," the general returned confidently. "She can't leave the town without being arrested. Now, as to our plan for Woodhouse's reception—this affair of Craigen's wife; we might as well agree on points, so that——" He heard his wife's voice in the room off the library, and broke off abruptly. "Confound it; the women are coming! Just step into my room with me, and we'll go over this little matter, Major."

General Crandall held open a small door at the left of his desk and followed Bishop through. Lady Crandall and Jane entered the library almost at the same time.

"This tea of George's is preposterous," the lady of Government House was grumbling. "Said we must have this man from Egypt here at once."

"If you were English, no tea could be preposterous," Jane countered, with a brave attempt at lightness. She felt each passing moment a weight adding to the suspense of the inevitable event.

"Well, I'm going to get it through with just as soon as I can," Lady Crandall snapped. Then Jaimihr Khan threw open the double doors and announced: "Cap-tain Wood-house, my lady!"

"Show him up!" she commanded; then in complaint to Jane: "Now where do you suppose that husband of mine went? Just like him to suggest a tea and forget to make an appearance."

Captain Woodhouse appeared between the opened doors in khaki and trim puttees. He stood very straight for an instant, his eyes

shooting rapidly about the room. Lady Crandall hurried forward to greet him, and his
momentary stiffness disappeared. The girl behind her followed slowly, almost reluctantly.
Woodhouse grasped her extended hand.

"It was good of you to send the flowers," she
murmured. The man smiled appreciation.

"Do you know," he said, "after I sent them
I thought you'd consider me a bit—prompt."

"I am learning something every day—about
Englishmen," Jane managed to answer, with a
ghost of a smile.

"Always something good, I hope," Woodhouse was quick to retort, his eyes eagerly trying to fathom the cause of the girl's restraint.

Lady Crandall, who had been vainly ringing
for Jaimihr Khan, excused herself on the necessity of looking after the tea things. Jane
experienced a quick stab of dread at finding
herself alone with this man. Unexpected opportunity was urging a decision which an hour
of solitude in her room had failed to bring.
Yet she trembled, appalled and afraid to speak,
before the very magnitude of the moment's exigency. "A spy—a spy!" whispered austere
duty. "He will die!" her heart cried in protest.

"Miss Gerson, it's good to see you again and know by your handclasp you have forgiven me for—for what was very necessary at the moment—last night—our meeting in the Splendide." Captain Woodhouse was standing before her now, his grave eyes looking down into hers. The girl caught a deep note of sincerity and something else—something vibrantly personal. Yet her tongue would not be loosed of its burden.

"A very pretty speech," she answered, with attempted raillery. "I shall think of it on the boat going home."

"I say, I wish you weren't always in that horrid state of mind—on your way home mentally," Captain Woodhouse challenged.

"I shall be so in reality day after to-morrow, I hope," she replied. "Away from all this bewildering war and back in comfortable little New York." The man seemed genuinely grieved at her announcement.

"New York must be worth while; but I imagine you have nothing picturesque—nothing old there. I'll wager you haven't a single converted monastery like Government House in all your city."

"Not many things in New York have been converted," she answered, with a smile. "Our greatest need is for a municipal evangelist."

False—all false, this banter! She knew it to be, and so she believed he must read it. And the man—his ease of manner was either that of innocence or of supreme nerve, the second not less to be admired than the first. Could it be that behind his serious eyes, now frankly telling her what she dared not let herself read in them, lay duplicity and a spy's cunning?

"I fancy you New Yorkers suffer most from newness—newness right out of the shop," she heard him saying. "But the old things are the best. Imagine the monks of a long-ago yesterday toasting themselves before this ancient fireplace." He waved toward the massive Gothic mantel bridging a cavernous fireplace. An old chime bell, green with weathering, hung on a low frame beside the firedogs.

"You're mistaken; that's manufactured antiquity," Jane caught him up. "Lady Crandall told me last night that fireplace is just five years old. One of the preceding governor's hobbies, it was."

Woodhouse caught at her answer with a

quick lifting of the brows. He turned again to feast his eyes on the girl's piquant face, even more alluring now because of the fleeting color that left the cheeks with a tea rose's coldness.

"Miss Gerson, something I have done or said"—the man was laboring after words—"you are not yourself, and maybe I am respon——"

She turned from him with a slight shudder. Her hand was extended in mute appeal for silence. He waited while his eyes followed the heaving of her shoulders under the emotion that was racking her. Suddenly she faced him again, and words rushed from her lips in an abandon of terror:

"Captain Woodhouse, I know too much—about you and why you are here. Oh, more than I want to! Accident—bad luck, believe me, it is not my seeking that I know you are a—a——"

He had started forward at her outburst, and now he stood very close to her, his gray eyes cold and unchanging.

"Say it—say the word! I'm not afraid to hear it," he commanded tensely. She drew back

from him a little wildly, her hands fluttering up
as if to fend him off.

"You—you are in great danger this minute.
You were brought here this afternoon to be
trapped—exposed and made——"

"I was fully aware of that when I came, Miss
Gerson," he interrupted. "The invitation, coming so suddenly—so pressing—I think I read it
aright."

"But the promise you made me give last
night!" Sudden resentment brushed aside for
the instant the girl's first flood of sympathy.
"That has involved me with you. Oh, that was
unfair—to make me promise I would not allude
to—to our first meeting!"

"Involved you?" He closed one of her hands
in his as if to calm her and force more rational
speech. "Then you have been——"

"Questioned by General Crandall—about
you," she broke in, struggling slightly to free
her hand. "Questioned—and even bullied and
threatened."

"And you kept your promise?" The question
was put so low Jane could hardly catch it. She
slowly nodded.

"Miss Gerson, you will never have cause to regret that you did." Woodhouse pressed her hand with almost fierce intenseness, then let it go. Her face was flaming now under the stress of excitement. She knew tears stood in her eyes, and was angered at their being there; he might mistake them. Woodhouse continued, in the same suppressed tone:

"You were on the point of using a word a minute ago, Miss Gerson, which was hard for you to voice because you thought it an ugly word. You seemed sure it was the right word to fit me. You only hesitated out of—ah—decency. Yet you kept faith with me before General Crandall. May I hope that means——"

"You may hope nothing!" Quick rebellion at what she divined to be coming flamed in Jane's eyes. "You have no right to hope for more from me than what you forced by promise. I would not be saying what I have to you if—if I did not feel I—that your life——"

"You misunderstood," he broke in stiffly. "I was on the point of saying I hoped you would not always believe me a——"

"Not believe!" Her hand went to the broad

ribbon belt she wore and brought out the silver cigarette case. This she passed to him with a swift gesture.

"Almer, the Hotel Splendide man, gave me this to-day at parade, urging that I deliver it to you." She was speaking hurriedly. "By a miracle—the strangest circumstance in the world— I learned the message this cigarette case was to carry to you. Oh, no, innocently enough on my part—it came by a chance I must not take the time to explain."

"A message from—Almer to me?" Woodhouse could not conceal the start her words gave him. He took a step toward her eagerly.

"Yes, a message. You must have it to protect yourself. The message was this:

"Informer has denounced you and Louisa to——"

Her voice died in her throat. Over Captain Woodhouse's shoulder she saw a door open. General Crandall and a short fat man in officer's uniform entered the library.

CHAPTER XV

THE THIRD DEGREE

"GOOD afternoon, Captain Woodhouse." General Crandall came forward and shook the captain's hand cordially. "Miss Gerson, Major Bishop, of my staff."

Jane acknowledged the introduction. Major Bishop advanced to the meeting with Woodhouse expectantly. With an air of ill-assumed ease, the governor made them known to each other.

"Major Bishop, your new man in the signal tower, Captain Woodhouse, from Wady Halfa. Captain, do you happen to remember the major? Was a captain when you were here on the Rock—captain in the engineers."

"I'm afraid we never met," Woodhouse began easily. "I was here such a short time. Expected to meet Major Bishop when I reported at his office this morning, but he was over at the wireless station, his aid told me."

"Right, Captain!" Bishop chirped, shaking his subordinate's hand. "I—ah—imagine this *is* the first time we've met." He put the least shade of emphasis on the verb.

Woodhouse met his eyes boldly. Lady Crandall, bustling in at this minute, directed a maid where to wheel the tea wagon, while Jane went to assist her with the pouring. The men soon had their cups, and the general and major contrived to group themselves with Woodhouse sitting between them. Sir George, affecting a gruff geniality, launched a question:

"Rock look familiar to you, Captain?"

"After a fashion, yes," Woodhouse answered slowly. "Though three months is so short a time for one to get a lasting impression."

"Nonsense!" the general reproved gustily. "Some places you see once you never forget. This old Rock is one of them; eh, Bishop?"

"I don't know," the chunky little officer replied. "The powers back home never give me a chance to get away and forget." There was a pause as the men sipped their tea. Woodhouse broke the silence:

"Man can be stationed in worse places than Gibraltar."

"If you mean Egypt, I agree with you," Crandall assented. "There six years."

"Were you, General? What station?" Woodhouse was coolly stirring his tea, emphatically at his ease. Jane, her back to the men as she fussed over the tea wagon, filled her own cup with hot water inadvertently. She tried to laugh over the mistake, but her fingers trembled as she poured the water back into the kettle.

"Not on the lazy old Nile, as you were—lucky dog!" the general returned. "Out on the yellow sands—at Arkowan—a place in the sun, never fear!"

The women had their cups now, and joined the men, sitting a little behind. Jane caught a shrewd sidewise glance from the general—a glance that sought a quick and sure reading of her emotions. She poised her cup as if expecting a question and the glance turned aside. But it had warned the girl that she was not altogether a passive factor in the situation. She set a guard over her features.

"Let me see, Captain Woodhouse"—it was little Bishop who took up the probe—"you must have been here in the days when Craigen was governor—saw your papers have it that you were here three months in nineteen seven."

"Yes, Craigen was governor then," Woodhouse answered guardedly.

"You never saw him, General." Bishop turned to Sir George. "Big, bluff, blustering chap, with a voice like the bull of Bashan. Woodhouse, here, he'll recognize my portrait."

Woodhouse smiled—secret disdain for the clumsy trap was in that smile.

"I'm afraid I do not," he said. "Craigen was considered a small, almost a delicate, man." He had recognized the bungling emphasis laid by Bishop on the Craigen characteristics, and his answer was pretty safely drawn by choosing the opposites. Bishop looked flustered for an instant, then admitted Woodhouse was right. He had confused Sir David Craigen with his predecessor, he said in excuse.

"I fancy I ought to remember the man. I had tea in this very room with him several times," Woodhouse ventured. He let his eyes rove as if in reminiscence. "Much the same here—as—except, General Crandall, I don't recall that fireplace." He indicated the heavy Gothic ornament on the opposite side of the room.

Jane caught her breath under the surge of secret elation. The resource of the man so to turn to advantage a fact that she had carelessly given him in their conversation of a few moments back! The girl saw a flicker of surprise cross General Crandall's face. Lady Crandall broke in:

"You have a good memory, after all, Captain Woodhouse. That fireplace is just five years old."

"Um—yes, yes," her husband admitted. "Clever piece of work, though. Likely to deceive anybody by its show of antiquity."

General Crandall called for a second slice of lemon in his cup. He was obviously sparring for another opening, but was impressed by the showing the suspected man was making. Bishop pushed the inquisition another step:

"Did you happen to be present, Captain, at the farewell dinner we gave little Billy Barnes? I think it must have been in the spring you were here."

"There were many dinners, Major Bishop." Woodhouse was carefully selecting his words, and he broke his sentences with a sip from his cup. "Seven years is a long time, you know.

We had much else to think about in Egypt than old dinners elsewhere."

Bishop appeared struck by an inspiration. He clapped his cup into its saucer with a sudden bang.

"Hang it, man, you must have been here in the days of Lady Evelyn. Remember her, don't you?"

"Would I be likely to forget?" the captain parried. Out of the tail of his eye he had a flash of Jane Gerson's white face, of her eyes seeking his with a palpitant, hunted look. The message of her eyes brought to him an instant of grace in sore trial.

"Seven years of Egypt—or of a hotter place —couldn't make a man forget her!" The major was rattling on for the benefit of those who had not come under the spell of the charmer. "Sir David Craigen's wife, and as lovely a woman as ever came out from England. Every man on the Rock lost his heart that spring. Woodhouse, even in three months' time you must have fallen like the rest of us."

"I'd rather not incriminate myself." Woodhouse smiled sagely as he passed his cup to Lady Crandall to be refilled.

"Don't blame you," Bishop caught him up. "A most outrageous flirt, and there was the devil to pay. Broken hearts were as thick on the Rock that year as strawberries in May, including poor Craigen's. And after one young subaltern tried to kill himself—you'll remember that, Woodhouse—Sir David packed the fair charmer off to England. Then he simply ate his heart out and—died."

"What an affecting picture!" Jane commented. "One lone woman capturing the garrison of Gibraltar!"

General Crandall rose to set his cup on the tea wagon. With the most casual air in the world, he addressed himself to Woodhouse:

"When Sir David died, many of his effects were left in this house to await their proper owner's disposition, and Lady Craigen has been —er—delicate about claiming them. Among them was the portrait of Lady Craigen herself which still hangs in this room. Have you recognized it, Captain?"

Woodhouse, whose mind had been leaping forward, vainly trying to divine the object of the Lady Evelyn lead, now knew, and the knowledge left him beyond his resources. He recognized the moment of his unmasking. But the man's nerve was steady, even in extremity. He rose and turned to face the rear wall of the library, against the tapestry of which hung four oil portraits in their deep old frames of heavy gold. Three of these were of women. A fourth, also the likeness of a woman, hung over the fireplace. Chances were four to one against blind choice.

As Woodhouse slowly lifted his eyes to the line of portraits, he noticed that Jane had moved to place the broad tent shade of a floor lamp on its tall standard of mahogany between herself and the other two men so that her face was momentarily screened from them. She looked quickly at the portrait over the mantel and away again. Woodhouse, knowing himself the object of two pairs of hostile eyes, made his survey deliberately, with purpose increasing the tension of the moment. His eyes ranged the line of portraits on the rear wall, then turned to that one over the fireplace.

"Ah, yes, a rather good likeness, eh, Major?" He drawled his identification with a disinterested air.

Crandall's manner underwent instant change.

His former slightly strained punctiliousness gave way to naturalness and easy spirits. One would have said he was advocate for a man on trial, for whom the jury had just pronounced, "Not proven." Scotch verdict, yes, but one acceptable enough to the governor of Gibraltar. The desk telephone sounded just then, and General Crandall answered. After listening briefly, he gave the orders, "Dress flags!" and hung up the receiver.

" 'Fleet's just entering the harbor,' signal tower reports," he explained to the others. "Miss Gerson, if you care to step here to the window you'll see something quite worth while."

Jane, light-hearted almost to the point of mild hysteria at the noticeable relaxation of strain denoting danger passed, bounded to a double French window giving on a balcony and commanding a view of all the bay to the Spanish shore. She exclaimed, in awe:

"Ships—ships! Hundreds of them! Why, General, what——"

"The Mediterranean fleet, young woman, bound home to protect the Channel against the German high-seas fleet." Deep pride was in the governor's voice. His eyes kindled as they fell

on the distant pillars of smoke—scores of them
mounting straight up to support the blue on
their blended arches. Captain Woodhouse could
scarcely conceal the start General Crandall's
announcement gave him. He followed the
others to the window more slowly.

"Wirelessed they'd be in ten hours ago," the
governor explained to his wife. "Rear-admiral
won't make his official call until morning, however. In these times he sticks by his flagship
after five o'clock."

"Wonderful—wonderful!" Bishop turned in
unfeigned enthusiasm to Woodhouse, behind
him. "There is the power—and the pride—of
England. Sort of thrills a chap, eh?"

"Rather!" Woodhouse replied.

"Well, must get down to the quay to receive
any despatches that may come ashore," the
major exclaimed. "Gad, but it gives me a little
homesick tug at the heart to see these grim old
dogs of war. They represent that tight little
island that rules the waves."

"Ah, London—London—the big, old town
where they pull the strings that make us
dance!" General Crandall, leaning against the

window frame, his eyes on the incoming fleet, voiced the chronic nostalgia of the man in the service.

"The town for me!" Woodhouse exclaimed with fervor. "I'm sick for the sight of her—the sounds of her—the smells of her: the orange peel and the asphalt and the gas coming in over Vauxhall Bridge."

Bishop turned on him admiringly.

"By George, that does hit it off, old man—no mistake!"

Jane was out on the balcony now with field glasses she had picked up from the governor's desk. She called back through the curtains, summoning Woodhouse to come and pick out for her the flagship. When he had joined her, Bishop stepped quickly to his superior's side.

"What do you think, General? By George, it seems to me it would need an Englishman to give one that sniff of London this chap just got off."

"Exactly," the general caught him up crisply. "And an Englishman's done it—Rudyard Kipling. Any German who can read English can read Kipling."

"But what do you think, General? Chap strikes me as genuine—that portrait of Lady Evelyn clenched things, I take it."

"Confound it! We haven't absolutely proved anything, pro or con," General Crandall grumbled, in perplexity. "Thing'll have to be decided by the Indian—what he finds, or doesn't find—in Woodhouse's room. Let you know soon as I hear."

Bishop hurried to make his adieux to Lady Crandall and her guest, and was starting for the doors when Woodhouse, stepping in from the balcony, offered to join him. The governor stopped him.

"By the way, Captain, if you'll wait for me a minute I should like your company down the Rock."

Bishop had gone, and the general, taking Woodhouse's agreement for granted, also left the room.

Woodhouse, suddenly thrown back on his guard, could find nothing to do but assent. But when Lady Crandall excused herself on the score of having to dress for dinner, he welcomed compensation in being alone with the girl who had gone with him steadfastly, unflinchingly, through moments of trial. She stood before the curtains screening the balcony, hesitant, apparently meditating flight. To her Woodhouse went, in his eyes an appeal for a moment alone which would not be denied.

"You were—very kind to me," he began, his voice very low and broken. "If it had not been —for your help, I would have——"

"I could not see you—see you grope blindly— and fail." She turned her head to look back through the opened glass doors to the swiftly moving dots in the distance that represented the incoming battle fleet.

"But was there no other reason except just humanity to prompt you?" He had possessed himself of one of her hands now, and his eyes compelled her to turn her own to meet their gaze. "Once when they—were trying to trip me, I caught a look from your eyes, and—and it was more than—than pity."

"You are presuming too much," the girl parried faintly; but Woodhouse would not be rebuffed.

"You must hear me," he rushed on impetuously. "This is a strange time for me to say this, but you say you are going—going away

soon. I may not have another opportunity—
hear me! I am terribly in earnest when I tell
you I love you—love you beyond all believing.
No, no! Not for what you have done for me,
but for what you are to me—beloved."

She quickly pulled her hand free from his
grasp and tried to move to the door. He blocked
her way.

"I can not have you go without a word from
you," he pleaded. "Just a word to tell me I
may——"

"How can you expect—that—I—knowing
what I do——" She was stumbling blindly,
but persisted: "You, who have deceived others,
are deceiving them now—how can I know you
are not deceiving me, too?"

"I can not explain." He dropped his head
hopelessly, and his voice seemed lifeless. "It
is a time of war. You must accept my word
that I am honest—with you."

She slowly shook her head and started again
for the double doors. "Perhaps—when you
prove that to me——." He took an eager step
toward her. "But, no, you can not. I will be
sailing so soon, and—and you must forget."

"You   ask   the   impossible!"   Woodhouse

quickly seized her hand and raised it to his lips. As he did so, the double doors opened noiselessly and Jaimihr Khan stood between them, sphinx-like.

Jane, startled, withdrew her hand, and without a farewell glance, ran across the library and through the door to Lady Crandall's room. Jaimihr Khan, with a cold glance at Woodhouse, moved silently to the door of General Crandall's room and knocked.

"It is I—Jaimihr Khan," he answered to the muffled hail from within. "Yes, General Sahib, I will wait."

He turned and looked toward Woodhouse. The latter had taken a cigarette from the case Almer had sent him through Jane, and was turning it over in his hand curiously. The Indian, treading like a hunting cat, began lighting candles. His tour of the room brought him to the captain's side, and there he stood, motionless, until Woodhouse, with a start, observed him.

"Cap-tain Wood-house has been most in-discreet," he said, in his curious mechanical way of speech.

Woodhouse turned on him angrily.

"What do you mean?" he snapped.

"Is it that they have ceased to teach discretion—at the Wilhelmstrasse?" The Indian's face was a mask.

"I know nothing about the Wilhelmstrasse," the white man answered, in a voice suddenly strained.

"Then it is veree, veree foolish for the captain to leave in his room these plans." Jaimihr Khan took from his girdle a thin roll of blue prints—the plans of the signal tower and Room D which Almer had given Woodhouse the night before. He held them gingerly between slender thumb and forefinger.

Woodhouse recoiled.

"The general sahib has sent me to search the cap-tain's room," the even voice of Jaimihr Khan ran on. "Behold the results of my journey!"

Woodhouse sent a lightning glance at the door leading to the governor's room, then stepped lightly away from the Indian and regarded him with hard calculating eyes.

"What do you propose to do—with those plans?"

"What should I do?" The white shoulders

Jaimihr Khan held the tip to his master's cigarette.

of the Indian went up in a shrug. "They will
stand you before a wall, Cap-tain Wood-house.
And fire. It is the price of in-discretion at a
time like this."

Woodhouse's right hand whipped back to his
holster, which hung from his sword belt, and
came forward again with a thick, short-bar-
reled weapon in it.

"Give me those plans, you yellow hound!"

"Shoot!" Jaimihr Khan smiled. "Add one
in-discretion to another. Shoot, my youthful
fool!"

The door to General Crandall's room opened,
and the general, in uniform evening dress,
stepped into the library. Woodhouse swiftly
slipped his revolver behind his back, though
keeping it ready for instant use.

"All ready, Captain. Smoke." The general
extended his cigarette case toward Woodhouse.

The latter smilingly declined, his eyes all the
while on the Indian, who stood by the corner
of the general's desk. Between the sleek
brown hands a tiny blue roll of paper was
twisting into a narrower wisp under the careless manipulation of thin fingers.

"Well, Jaimihr," Crandall briskly addressed

the servant, "have you completed the errand I sent you on?"

"Yes, General Sahib." The brown fingers still caressed the plans of the signal tower.

"Have you anything to report?" The general had his cigarette in his mouth and was pawing his desk for a match. Jaimihr Khan slowly lifted the tip of the paper wisp in his fingers to the flame of a candle on the end of the desk, then held the burning tip to his master's cigarette.

"Nothing, General Sahib."

"Very good. Come, Woodhouse; sorry to have kept you waiting." The general started for the double doors. Woodhouse followed. He passed very close to the Indian, but the latter made no sign. His eyes were on the burning wisp of paper between his fingers.

CHAPTER XVI

THE PENDULUM OF FATE

THE next day, Thursday, was one of hectic excitement for Gibraltar. Focus of the concentrated attention of town and Rock was the battle fleet, clogging all the inner harbor with its great gray hulks. Superdreadnaughts, like the standing walls of a submerged Atlantis, lay close to the quays, barges lashed alongside the folded booms of their torpedo nets. Behind them, battle cruisers and scouts formed a protecting cordon. Far out across the entrance to the harbor, the darting black shapes of destroyers on constant guard were shuttles trailing their threads of smoke through the blue web of sea and sky. Between fleet and shore snorting cockleshells of launches established lanes of communication; khaki of the Rock's defenders and blue of the fleet's officers met, passed, and repassed. In wardroom and club lounge glasses were touched in pledges to the united service. The high commander of the Mediterranean fleet paid his official visit to the governor of Gibraltar, and the governor, in turn, was received with honors upon the quarterdeck of the flagship. But under the superficial courtesies of fanfare and present arms the stern business of coaling fleet progressed at high tension. It was necessary that all of the fighting machines have their bunkers filled by noon of the following day. Every minute that the Channel up under the murky North Sea fogs lay without full strength of her fleet protection was added danger for England.

That morning, Captain Woodhouse went on duty in the signal tower. Major Bishop, his superior, had summoned him to his office immediately after breakfast and assigned him to his tasks there. Sufficient proof, Woodhouse assured himself, with elation, that he had come through the fire in General Crandall's library, tested and found genuine. Through this pretext and that, he had been kept off duty the day before, denied access to the slender stone tower high up on the Rock's crest which was the motor center of Gibraltar's ganglia of defense.

The small office in which Woodhouse was installed was situated at the very top of the tower—a room glassed on four sides like the lantern room of a lighthouse, and provided with telescope, a telephone switchboard, range finders, and all the complicated machinery of gun-fire control. On one side were trestle boards supporting charts of the ranges—figured areas representing every square yard of water from the nearer harbor below out to the farthest reaching distance of the monster disappearing guns. A second graphic sheet showed the harbor and anchorages and the entrance to the straits; this map was thickly spotted with little, red, numbered dots—the mines. Sown like a turnip field with these deadly capsules of destruction were all the waters thereabouts; their delicate tendrils led under water and through conduits in the Rock up to this slender spire called the signal tower. As he climbed the winding stairway to his newly assigned post, Woodhouse had seen painted on a small wooden door just below the room he was to occupy the single white letter "D."

Room D—where the switches were, where a single sweep of the hand could loose all the hidden death out there in the crowded harbor —it lay directly below his feet.

Captain Woodhouse's duties were not arduous. He had as single companion a sergeant of the signal service, whose post was at the window overlooking the harbor. The sergeant read the semaphore message from the slender signal arm on the flagship's bridge—directions for the coal barges' movements, businesslike orders to be transmitted to the quartermaster in charge of the naval stores ashore, and such humdrum of routine. These Woodhouse recorded and forwarded to their various destinations over the telephone.

He had much time for thought—and much to think about.

Yesterday's scene in the library of Government House—his grilling by the two suspicious men, when a false answer on his part would have been the first step toward a firing squad. Yes, and what had followed between himself and the little American—the girl who had protected and aided him—ah, the pain of that trial was hardly less poignant than had been the terror of the one preceding it. She had asked him to prove to her that he was not what she thought him. Before another day was past she would be out of his life and would depart, be-

lieving—yes, convinced—that the task he had
set himself to do was a dishonorable one. She
could not know that the soldiers of the Hidden
Army have claim to heroism no less than they
who join battle under the sun. But he was
to see Jane Gerson once more; Woodhouse
caught at this circumstance as something precious. To-night at Government House Lady
Crandall's dinner to the refugee Americans on
the eve of their departure would offer a last
opportunity. How could he turn it to the desire of his heart?

One more incident of a crowded yesterday
gave Woodhouse a crust for rumination—the
unmasking Jaimihr Khan, the Indian, had
elected for himself at that critical minute when
it lay in his power to betray the stranger in
the garrison. The captain reviewed the incident with great satisfaction—how of a sudden
the wily Indian had changed from an enemy
holding a man's life in his hand to that "friend
in Government House," of whose existence the
cautious Almer had hinted but whose identity
he had kept concealed. Almer had said that
this "friend" could lay his hand on the combination to Room D in the signal tower when the

proper moment arrived. Now that he knew
Jaimihr Khan in his true stripe, Woodhouse
made no doubt of his ability to fulfill Almer's
prophecy.

And the proper moment would be this night!
To-night, on the eve of the great fleet's sailing, what Woodhouse had come to Gibraltar
to do must be accomplished or not at all.

The man's nerves were taut, and he rose to
step to the bayward window, there to look
down on the embattled splendor of England's
defense. Steel forts ranged all in rows, awaiting but the opportunity to loose their lightnings
of obliteration against the ships of an enemy.
Cardboard ships! Shadows of dreams! In
Room D, just below his feet, a hand on the
switches—a downward push, and then——

Lady Crandall's dinner in Government House
was in full tide of hilarity. Under the heavy
groined ceiling the spread table with its napery
and silver was the one spot of light in the
long shadowed dining-room. Round it sat the
refugees—folk who had eaten black bread and
sausage and called that a meal; who had dodged
and twisted under the careless scourge of a

war beyond their understanding and sympa-
thies, ridden in springless carts, been bullied
and hectored by military martinets and beg-
gared by panicky banks. Now, with the first
glimpse of freedom already in sight and under the warming influence of an American hostess' real American meal, they were swept off
their feet by high spirits almost childlike.
Henry J. Sherman, Kewanee's vagrant son returning from painful pilgrimage, sat at the
right of Lady Crandall; his pink face was
glowing with humor. To Consul Reynolds, who
swore he would have to pay for thus neglect-
ing his consulate for so much as two hours,
had fallen the honor of escorting Mrs. Sherman
to table. Willy Kimball, polished as to shirt
bosom and sleek hair, had eyes and ears for
none but the blithe Kitty. Next to General
Crandall sat Jane Gerson, radiant in a dinner
gown of tricky gauze overlaid on silk. At her
right was Captain Woodhouse, in proper uniform dinner coat faced with red and gold. Of
the whole company, Woodhouse alone appeared
constrained. The girl by his side had been
cool in her greeting that evening; to his con-
versational sallies she had answered with in-

difference, and now at table she divided her favors between General Crandall and the perky little consul across the table. It seemed to Woodhouse that she purposely added a lash of cruelty to her joy at the approaching departure on the morrow.

"Oh, you must all listen to this!" Kitty Sherman commanded the attention of the table, with a clapping of hands. "Go ahead, Will; he had the funniest accident — tell them about it."

Young Kimball looked conscious and began to stammer.

"You're getting us all excited, Willy," Henry J. boomed from the opposite side of the table. "What happened?"

"Why — ah — really quite ridiculous, you know. Hardly a matter to—ah—talk about." Willy fumbled the rose in the lapel of his jacket and searched for words. "You see, this morning I was thinking very hard about what I would do when I got back to Kewanee—oh, quite enthusiastic I am about the little town, now—and I—well, I mean to say, I got into my bath with my wrist watch on."

Shouts of laughter added to the youth's confusion. Sherman leaned far across the table and advised him in a hoarse whisper:

"Buy a dollar Ingersoll, Willy. It floats!"

"Well, you might give him one of yours, father," Kitty put in, in quick defense. "Anybody who'd carry two watches around——"

"Two watches?" Lady Crandall was interested.

Henry J. beamed expansively, pulled away his napkin, and proudly lifted from each waistcoat pocket a ponderous watch, linked by the thick chain passing through a buttonhole.

"This one"—he raised the right-hand timepiece—"tells the time of the place I happen to be in—changed it so often I guess the works'll never be the same again. But this one is my pet. Here's Kewanee time—not touched since we pulled out of the C., B. & Q. station on the twentieth of last May." He turned the face around for the others to read. "Just three in the afternoon there now. Old Ed Porter's got the *Daily Enterprise* out on the street, and he's tilted back in his office chair, readin' the Chicago *Tribune* that's just got in on the two-five train. The boys at the bank are goin' out to the country club for golf—young

Pete Andrews wearin' the knickerbockers his wife cut down from his old overcoat; sort of a horse-blanket pattern, you might say. The town's just dozin' in the afternoon sun and—and not givin' a hang whether Henry J. Sherman and family gets back or not."

"You're an old dear!" Lady Crandall bubbled. "Some day Kewanee will erect a statue to you."

The talk turned to art, and the man from Kewanee even had the stolid general wiping the tears from his eyes by his description and criticism of some of the masters his wife had trotted him around to admire.

"Willy, you'll be interested to know we got a painter in Kewanee now," Henry J. cried. "'Member young Frank Coales—old Henry Coales' son? Well, he turned out to be an artist. Too bad, too; his folks was fine people. But Frank was awfully headstrong about art. Painted a war picture about as big as that wall there. Couldn't find a buyer right away, so he turned it over to Tim Burns, who keeps the saloon on Main Street. Been busy ever since, sorta taking it out in trade, you might say."

Table talk was running at a gay rate when Mrs. Sherman, who had sent frequent searching glances at Captain Woodhouse over the nodding buds of the flower piece in the center of the board, suddenly broke out:

"Ah, Captain Woodhouse, now I remember where I've seen you before! I thought your face was familiar the minute I set my eyes on you this evening."

Jaimihr Khan, who stood behind the general's chair, arms folded and motionless, swiftly lifted one hand to his lips, but immediately mastered himself again. General Crandall looked up with a sharp crinkle of interest between his eyes. Captain Woodhouse, unperturbed, turned to the Kewanee dowager.

"You have seen me before, Mrs. Sherman?"

"I am sure of it," the lady announced, with decision. The other diners were listening now.

"Indeed! And where?" Woodhouse was smiling polite attention.

"Why, at the Winter Garden, in Berlin—a month ago!" Mrs. Sherman was hugely satisfied with her identification. She appealed to her husband for confirmation. "Remember, father, that gentleman I mistook for Albert

Downs, back home, that night we saw that—
er—wicked performance?"

"Can't say I do," Sherman answered toler-
antly.

Woodhouse, still smiling, addressed Mrs.
Sherman:

"Frightfully sorry to disappoint you, Mrs.
Sherman, but I was not in Berlin a month ago.
I came here from Egypt, where I had been
several years." Woodhouse heard Jane at his
elbow catch her breath.

"See, mother, there you go on your old hobby
of recognizin' folks," Sherman chided. Then,
to the others: "Why, she's seen all Kewanee
since she came here to Europe. Even got a
glimpse of the Methodist minister at Monte
Carlo."

"I have never been in Berlin in my life, Mrs.
Sherman," Woodhouse was adding. "So, of
course——"

"Well, I suppose I am wrong," the lady admitted. "But still I could swear."

The governor, who had kept a cold eye on
his subordinate during this colloquy, now
caught Woodhouse's glance. The captain
smiled frankly.

"Another such unexpected identification, General, and you'll have me in the cells as a spy, I dare say," he remarked.

"Quite likely," Crandall answered shortly, and took up his fork again. A maid stepped to Lady Crandall's chair at this juncture and whispered something. The latter spoke to Woodhouse:

"You're wanted on the telephone in the library, Captain. Very important, so the importunate person at the other end of the wire informs the maid."

Woodhouse looked his confusion.

"Probably that silly ass at the quay who lost a bag of mine when I landed," he apologized, as he rose. "If you'll pardon me——"

Woodhouse passed up the stairs and into the library. He was surprised to find Jaimihr Khan standing by the telephone, his hand just in the act of setting the receiver back on the hook. The Indian stepped swiftly to the double doors and shut them behind the captain.

"A thousand pardons, Cap-tain"—he spoke hurriedly—"the cap-tain will stand near the telephone. They may come from the dining-room at any minute."

"What is all this?" Woodhouse began. "I was called on the telephone."

"A call I had inspired, Cap-tain. It was necessary to see you—at once and alone."

"Tactless! With the general suspecting me —you heard what that woman from America said at the table—she has eyes in her head!"

"I think he still. trusts you, Cap-tain," the Indian replied. "And to-night we must act. The fleet sails at noon to-morrow."

"We?" Woodhouse was on his guard at once. "What do you mean by 'we'?"

Jaimihr Khan smiled at the evasion.

"Yesterday in this room, Cap-tain, I burned a roll of plans——"

"Which I had good reason to wish saved," Woodhouse caught him up.

"No matter; I burned them—at a moment when you were—in great peril, Cap-tain."

"Burned them, yes—perhaps to trap me further."

The Indian made a gesture of impatience. "Oh, excellent discretion!" he cried in suppressed exasperation. "But we waste time that is precious. To-night——"

"Before another word is spoken, let me have

your card—your Wilhelmstrasse number,"
Woodhouse demanded.

"I carry no card. I am more discreet than
—some," the other answered insinuatingly.

"No card? Your number, then?"

Jaimihr Khan brought his lips close to the
white man's ear and whispered a number.

"Is that not correct?" he asked.

Woodhouse nodded curtly.

"And now that we are properly introduced,"
Jaimihr began, with a sardonic smile, "may I
venture a criticism? Your pardon, Cap-tain;
but our critics, they help us to per-fection.
Since when have men who come from the
Wilhelmstrasse allowed themselves to make
love in drawing-rooms?"

"You mean——"

"You and the young woman from America
—when I found you together here yesterday——"

"That is my affair," was Woodhouse's hot
response.

"The affair on which we work—this night—
that is *my* affair, be veree sure!" There was
something of menace in the Indian's tone.

Woodhouse bowed to his demand for an explanation. "That young woman, as it happens, must be kept on our side. She saw me in France, when Captain Woodhouse was supposed to be in Egypt."

"Ah, so?" Jaimihr inclined his head with a slight gesture craving pardon. "For that reason you make a conquest. I did not un-der-stand."

"No matter. The fleet sails at noon."

"And our moment is here—to-night," Jaimihr whispered in exultation. "Not until to-day did they admit you to the tower, Cap-tain. How is it there?"

"A simple matter—with the combination to the door of Room D."

With a single stride the Indian was over before the door of the wall safe. He pointed.

"The combination of the inner door—it is in a special compartment of that safe, protected by many wires. Before dawn I cut the wires —and come to you with the combination."

"At whatever hour is best for you," Woodhouse put in eagerly.

"Let us say three-thirty," Jaimihr answered. "You will be waiting for me at the Hotel Splendide with—our friends there. I shall come to you there, give you the combination, and you shall go through the lines to the signal tower."

"There must be no slip," Woodhouse sternly warned.

"Not on my part, Cap-tain—count on that. For five years I have been waiting—waiting. Five years a servant—yes, my General; no, my General; very good, my General." The man's voice vibrated with hate. "To-morrow, near dawn—the English fleet shattered and ablaze in the harbor—the water red, like blood, with the flames. Then, by the breath of Allah, my service ends!"

Voices sounded in the hallway outside the double doors. Jaimihr Khan, a finger to his lips, nodded as he whispered: "Three-thirty, at the Splendide." He faded like a white wraith through the door to General Crandall's room as the double doors opened and the masculine faction of the dinner party entered. Woodhouse rose from a stooping position at the telephone and faced them. To the general, whose sharp scrutiny stabbed like thin knives, he made plausible explanation. The beggar who lost his bag wanted a complete identification of it—had run it down at Algeciras.

"I understand," Crandall grunted.

When the cigars were lit, General Crandall excused himself for a minute, sat at his desk, and hurriedly scratched a note. Summoning Jaimihr, he ordered that the note be despatched by orderly direct to Major Bishop and given to no other hands. Woodhouse, who overheard his superior officer's command, was filled with vague apprehension. What Mrs. Sherman had said at table—this hurried note to Bishop; there was but one interpretation to give to the affair—Crandall's suspicions were all alive again. Yet at three-thirty—at the Hotel Splendide——

But when Crandall came back to join the circle of smokers, he was all geniality. The women came in by way of Jane Gerson's room; they had been taking a farewell peek at her dazzling stock of gowns, they said, before they were packed for the steamer.

"There was one or two I just had to see again," Mrs. Sherman explained for the benefit of all, "before I said good-by to them. One of them, by Madam Paquin, father, I'm going to copy when we get home. I'll be the first to introduce a Paquin into little Kewanee."

"Well, don't get into trouble with the minister, mother," Henry J. warned. "Some of the French gowns I've seen on this trip certainly would stir things up in Kewanee."

Jaimihr served the coffee. Woodhouse tried to maneuver Jane into a tête-à-tête in an angle of the massive fireplace, but she outgeneraled him, and the observant Mrs. Sherman cornered him inexorably.

"Tell me, Captain Woodhouse," she began, in her friendly tones, "you said a while ago the general might mistake you for a spy. Don't you have a great deal of trouble with spies in your army in war time? Everybody took us for spies in Germany, and in France they thought poor Henry was carrying bombs to blow up the Eiffel Tower."

"Perhaps I can answer that question better than Captain Woodhouse," the general put in, rising and striding over to where Mrs. Sherman kept the captain prisoner. "Captain Woodhouse, you see, would not be so likely to come in touch with those troublesome persons as one in command of a post, like myself." The most delicate irony barbed this speech, lost to all but the one for whom it was meant.

"Oh, I know I'm going to hear something very exciting," Mrs. Sherman chortled. "Kitty, you'd better hush up Willy Kimball for a while and come over here. You can improve your mind better listening to the general."

Crandall soon was the center of a group. He began, with sober directness.

"Well, in the matter of spies in war time, Mrs. Sherman, one is struck by the fact of their resemblance to the plague—you never can tell when they're going to get you or whence they came. Now here on the Rock I have reason to believe we have one or more spies busy this minute."

Jane Gerson, sitting where the light smote her face, drew back into the shadow with a swift movement of protectiveness. Woodhouse, who balanced a dainty Satsuma coffee cup on his knee, kept his eyes on his superior's face with a mildly interested air.

"In fact," Crandall continued evenly, "I shouldn't be surprised if one—possibly two spies—should be arrested before the night is over. And the point about this that will interest you ladies is that one of these—the one whose order for arrest I have already given—

is a woman—a very clever and pretty woman, I may add, to make the story more interesting."

"And the other, whose arrest may follow, is an accomplice of hers, I take it, General!" Woodhouse put the question with easy indifference. He was stirring his coffee abstractedly.

"Not only the accomplice, but the brains for both, Captain. A deucedly clever person, I'm frank to admit."

"Oh, people! Come and see the flagship, signaling to the rest of the fleet with its funny green and red lights!" It was Jane who had suddenly risen and stood by the curtains screening the balcony windows. "They look like little flowers opening and shutting."

The girl's diversion was sufficient to take interest momentarily from General Crandall's revelation. When all had clustered around the windows, conversation skipped to the fleet, its power, and the men who were ready to do battle behind its hundreds of guns. Mrs. Sherman was disappointed that the ships did not send up rockets. She'd read somewhere that ships sent up rockets, and she didn't see why these should prove the exception. Interruption came from Jaimihr Khan, who bore a message for Consul Reynolds. The fussy little man ripped open the envelope with an air of importance.

"Ah, listen, folks! Here we have the latest wireless from the *Saxonia.* 'Will anchor about two—sail six. Have all passengers aboard by five-thirty.'" Excited gurgles from the refugees. "That means," Reynolds wound up, with a flourish, "everybody at the docks by five o'clock. Be there myself, to see you off. Must go now—lot of fuss and feathers getting everybody fixed." He paused before Jane.

"You're going home at last, young lady," he chirped.

"That depends entirely on Miss Gerson herself." It was the general who spoke quietly but emphatically.

Reynolds looked at him, surprised.

"Why, I understood it was all arranged——"

"I repeat, it depends entirely on Miss Gerson."

Woodhouse caught the look of fear in Jane's eyes, and, as they fell for the instant on his, something else—appeal. He turned his head quickly. Lady Crandall saved the situation.

"Oh, that's just some more of George's eternal red tape. I'll snip it when the time comes."

The consul's departure was the signal for the others. They crowded around Lady Crandall and her husband with voluble praise for the American dinner and thanks for the courtesy they had found on the Rock. Woodhouse, after a last despairing effort to have a word of farewell with Jane, which she denied, turned to make his adieu to his host and hostess.

"No hurry, Captain," Crandall caught him up. "Expect Major Bishop in every minute— small matter of official detail. You and he can go down the Rock together when he leaves."

Woodhouse's mind leaped to the meaning behind his superior's careless words. The hastily despatched note—that was to summon Bishop to Government House; Crandall's speech about the two spies and the arrest of one of them— Louisa, he meant—and now this summary order that he wait the arrival of Bishop—would the second arrest be here in this room? The man who carried a number from the Wilhelmstrasse felt the walls of the library slowly closing in to crush him; he could almost hear the whisper and mutter of the inexorable machine moving them closer—closer. Be alone with the man whose word could send bullets into his heart!

"A very pleasant dinner—Lady Crandall's," Woodhouse began, eager to lighten the tenseness of the situation.

"Yes, it seemed so." Crandall offered the younger man his cigarette case, and, lighting a smoke himself, straddled the hearth, his eyes keenly observant of Woodhouse's face.

"Rather odd, Americans. But jolly nice." The captain laughed in reminiscence of the unspoiled Shermans.

"I thought so—I married one," Crandall retorted.

The ear of Woodhouse's mind could hear more plainly now the grinding of the cogs; the immutable power of fate lay there.

"Oh—er—so you did. Very kind she has been to me. I got very little of this sort of thing at Wady Halfa."

"By the way, Woodhouse"—Crandall blew a contemplative puff toward the ceiling—"strange Mrs. Sherman should have thought she saw you at Berlin."

"Odd mistake, to be sure," Woodhouse admitted, struggling to put ease into his voice. "The lady seems to have a penchant, as her husband says, for finding familiar faces."

"Major Bishop!" Jaimihr Khan announced at the double doors. The major in person followed immediately. His greeting to Woodhouse was constrained.

"Woodhouse will wait for you to go down the Rock with him," Crandall explained to the newcomer. "Captain, excuse us for a minute, while we go into my room and run over a little matter of fleet supplies. Must check up with the fleet before it sails in the morning." Woodhouse bowed his acquiescence and saw the door to the general's room close behind the twain.

He was not long alone. Noiselessly the double doors opened and Jaimihr Khan entered. Woodhouse sprang to meet him where he stood poised for flight just inside the doors.

"The woman's prattle of Berlin——" the Indian whispered.

"Yes, the general's suspicions are all aroused again."

"Listen! I saw the note he sent to Bishop. The major is to be set to watch you to-night— all night. A false step and you will be under arrest." Jaimihr's thin face was twisted in wrath. "One man's life will not stand in our way now."

"No," Woodhouse affirmed.

"Success is veree near. When Bishop goes with you down the Rock——"

"Yes, yes! What?"

"The pistol screams, but the knife is dumb. Quick, Cap-tain!" With a swift movement of his hand the Indian passed a thin-bladed dirk to the white man. The latter secreted the sheathed weapon in a pocket of his dinner jacket. He nodded understanding.

"One man's life—nothing!" Jaimihr breathed.

"It shall be done," Woodhouse whispered.

Jaimihr faded through the double doors like a spirit in a medium's cabinet. He had seen what the captain was slower to notice. The door from Jane Gerson's room was opening. The girl stepped swiftly into the room, and was by Woodhouse's side almost before he had seen her.

"I could not—go away—without—without——"

"Miss Gerson—Jane!" He was beside her instantly. His hand sought and found one of hers and held it a willing prisoner. She was trembling, and her eyes were deep pools, riffled by conflicting currents. Her words came breathlessly:

"I was not myself—I tried to tell myself you were deceiving me just—just as a part of this terrible mystery you are involved in. But when I heard General Crandall tell you to wait—that and what he said about the spies—I knew you were again in peril, and—and——"

"And you have come to me to tell me as goodby you believe I am honest and that you care—a little?" Woodhouse's voice trembled with yearning. "When you think me in danger, then you forget doubts and maybe—your heart——"

"Oh, I want to believe—I want to!" she whispered passionately. "Every one here is against you. Tell me you are on the level—with me, at least."

"I am—with you."

"I—believe," she sighed, and her head fell near his shoulder—so near that with alacrity Captain Woodhouse settled it there.

"When this war is over, if I am alive," he was saying rapturously, "may I come to America for you? Will you—wait?"

"Perhaps."

The door to General Crandall's room opened. They sprang apart just as Crandall and Bishop entered the library. The former was not blind to the situation; he darted a swift glance into the girl's face and read much there.

"Ready, Captain?" Bishop chirped, affecting not to notice the momentary confusion of the man and the girl.

Woodhouse gave Jane's hand a lingering clasp; mutely his eyes adjured her to remember her plighted troth. In another minute he was gone.

The general and his guest were alone. Jane Gerson was bidding him good night when he interrupted, somewhat gruffly:

"Well, young woman, have you made up your mind? Do you sail in the morning—or not?"

"I made up my mind to that long ago," she answered briskly. "Of course I sail."

"Then you're going to tell me what I want to know. Sensible girl!" He rubbed his hands in satisfaction.

"What is it you want to know, General Crandall?" This almost carelessly from her.

"When did you meet Woodhouse before—and where?"

"How do you know I met him before?" She attempted to parry, but Crandall cut her short with a gesture of impatience:

"Please don't try that tack again. Answer those two questions, and you sail in the morning."

Jane Gerson's eyes grew hard, and she lifted her chin in defiance.

"And if I refuse——"

"Why should you?" Crandall affected surprise not altogether unfelt.

"No matter—I do!" The challenge came crisp and sharp-cut as a new blade. Gibraltar's governor lost his temper instanter; his face purpled.

"And I know why!" he rasped. "He's got round you—made love to you—tricked you! I'd swear he was kissing you just the minute I came in here. The German cad! Good lord, girl; can't you see how he's using you?"

"I'm afraid I can't."

Crandall advanced toward her, shaking a menacing finger at her.

"Let me tell you something, young woman: he's at the end of his rope. Done for! No use for you to stand up for him longer. He's under guard to-night, and a woman named Josepha, his accomplice—or maybe his dupe—is already under arrest, and to-morrow, when we examine her, she'll reveal his whole rotten schemes or have to stand against a wall with him. Come, now! Throw him over. Don't risk your job, as you call it, for a German spy who's tricked you—made a fool of you. Why——"

"General Crandall!" Her face was white, and her eyes glowed with anger.

"I—I beg your pardon, Miss Gerson," he mumbled. "I am exasperated. A fine girl like you—to throw away all your hopes and ambitions for a spy—and a bounder! Can't you see you're wrong?"

"General Crandall, some time—I hope it will be soon—you will apologize to me—and to Captain Woodhouse—for what you are saying to-night." Her hands clenched into fists, whereon the knuckles showed white; the poise of her head, held a little forward, was all combative.

"Then you won't tell me what I want to

know?" He could not but read the defiance in the girl's pose.

"I will tell you nothing but good-by."

"No, by gad—you won't! I can be stubborn, too. You shan't sail on the *Saxonia* in the morning. Understand?"

"Oh, shan't I? Who will dare stop me?"

"I will, Miss Gerson. I have plenty of right—and the power, too."

"I'll ask you to tell that to my consul—on the dock at five to-morrow morning. Until then, General Crandall, au revoir."

The door of the guest room shut with a spiteful slam upon the master of Gibraltar, leaving him to nurse a grievance on the knees of wrath.

CHAPTER XVII

JOSEPH ALMER and Captain Woodhouse
sat in the darkened and heavily blinded
office-reception room of the Hotel Splendide.
All the hotel had long since been put to bed,
and the silence in the rambling house was audi-
ble. The hands of the Dutch clock on the wall
were pointing to the hour of three-thirty.

Strain was on both the men. They spoke in
monosyllables, and only occasionally. Almer's
hand went out from time to time to lift a squat
bottle of brandy from the table between them
and pour a tiny glass brimful; he quaffed with
a sucking noise. Woodhouse did not drink.

"It is three-thirty," the latter fretted, with
an eye on the mottled clock dial.

"He will come," Almer assured. A long
pause.

"This man Jaimihr—he is thoroughly dependable?" The man in uniform put the question with petulant bruskness.

"It is his passion—what we are to do to-night—something he has lived for—his religion. Nothing except judgment day could—— Hah!"

The sharp chirp of a telephone bell, a dagger of sound in the silence, broke Almer's speech. He bounded to his feet; but not so quickly as Woodhouse, who was across the room in a single stride and had the receiver to his ear.

"Well, well! Yes, this is the one you name." Woodhouse turned to Almer, and his lips framed the word Jaimihr. "Yes, yes; all is well—and waiting. Bishop? He is beyond interference—coming down the Rock—I did the work silently. What's that?" Woodhouse's face was tensed in strain; his right hand went to a breast pocket and brought out a pencil. With it he began making memoranda on the face of a calendar by his side.

"Seven turns—ah, yes—four to the left—correct." His writing hand was moving swiftly. "Press, one to the right. Good! I have it, and am off at once. Good-by!"

Woodhouse finished a line of script on the calendar face, hung up the receiver. He carefully tore the written notes from the calendar and put them into his pocket.

"Jaimihr says he has work to do at Government House and can not come down." Woodhouse turned to Almer and explained in rapid sentences. "But he's given me the combination —to Room D—over the wire, and now I'm off!"

Almer was all excitement now. He hovered lovingly about Woodhouse, patting him on the shoulder, giving him his helmet, mothering him with little cooing noises.

"Speed quickly, Nineteen Thirty-two! Up the Rock to the signal tower, Nineteen Thirty-two, to do the deed that will boom around the world. The switches—one pull, my brother, and the fatherland is saved to triumph over her enemies, victorious!"

"Right, Almer!" Woodhouse was moving toward the door. "In eight minutes history will be made. The minute you hear the blast, start for Spain. I will try to escape, but I doubt——"

A knock came at the barred front door— one knock, followed by three. Both men were transfixed. Almer, first to recover his calmness, motioned Woodhouse through the door to the dining-room. When his companion had disappeared, he stepped to the door and cautiously asked: "Who knocks?"

An answer came that caused him to shoot back the bolts and thrust out his head. A message was hurriedly whispered into his ear. The Splendide's proprietor withdrew his head and slipped the bolt home again. His face was a thundercloud as he summoned Woodhouse; his breath came in wheezy gasps.

"My Arab boy comes to the door just now to tell me of Louisa's fate; she has been arrested," he said.

"Come, Almer! I am going to the signal tower—there is still time for us to strike."

Out on to Waterport Street leaped Woodhouse, and the door closed behind him.

CHAPTER XVIII

THE TRAP IS SPRUNG

JANE GERSON, tossing on her pillows, heard the mellow bell of a clock somewhere in the dark and silent house strike three. This was the fifth time she had counted the measured strokes of that bell as she lay, wide-eyed, in the guest chamber's canopied bed. An eternity had passed since the dinner guests' departure. Her mind was racing like some engine gone wild, and sleep was impossible. Over and over again she had conned the events of the evening, always to come at the end against the impasse of General Crandall's blunt denial: "You shan't sail in the morning." In her extremity she had even considered flight by stealth—the scaling of walls perhaps, and a groping through dark streets to the wharf, there to smuggle herself somehow on a tender and so gain the *Saxonia*. But her precious gowns! They still reposed in their bulky hampers here in Government House; to escape and leave them behind would be worse than futile. The governor's fiat seemed absolute.

Urged by the impulse of sheer necessity to be doing something—the bed had become a rack —the girl rose, lit a taper, and began to dress herself, moving noiselessly. She even packed her traveling bag to the last inch and locked it. Then she sat on the edge of the bed, hands helplessly folded in her lap. What to do next? Was she any better off dressed than thrashing in the bed? Her yearning called up a picture of the *Saxonia*, which must ere this be at her anchorage, since the consul said she was due at two. In three short hours tenders would puff alongside; a happy procession of refugees climb the gangway—among them the Shermans and Willy Kimball, bound for their Kewanee; the captain on the bridge would give an order; winches would puff, the anchor heave from the mud, the big boat's prow slowly turn westward — oceanward — toward New York! And she, a prisoner caught by the mischance of war's great mystery, would have to watch that diminishing column of smoke fade against the morning's blue—disappear.

Inspiration seized her. It would be something just to see the *Saxonia,* now lying amid the grim monsters of the war fleet. From the balcony of the library, just outside the door of her room, she could search the darkness of the harbor for the prickly rows of lights marking the merchant ship from her darker neighbors. The general's marine glasses lay on his desk, she remembered. To steal out to the balcony, sweep the harbor with the glasses, and at last hit on the ship of deliverance—for all but her; to do this would be better than counting the hours alone. She softly opened the door of her room. Beyond lay the dim distances of the library, suddenly become vast as an amphitheater; in the thin light filtering through the curtains screening the balcony appeared the lumpy masses of furniture and vague outlines of walls and doors. She closed the door behind her, and stood trembling; this was somehow like burglary, she felt—at least it had the thrill of burglary.

The girl tiptoed around a high-backed chair, groped her way to the general's desk, and fumbled there. Her hand fell upon the double tubes of the binoculars. She picked them up,

parted the curtains, and stepped through the
opened glass doors to the balcony. Not a sound
anywhere but the faint cluck and cackle of
cargo hoists down in the harbor. Jane put the
glasses to her eyes, and began to sweep the
light-pointed vista below the cliff. Scores of
pin-prick beams of radiance marked the fleet
where it choked the roadstead—red and white
beetles' eyes in the dark. She swung the glasses
nearer shore. Ah, there lay the *Saxonia,* with
her three rows of glowing portholes near the
water; the binoculars even picked out the
double column of smoke from her stacks.
Three brief hours and that mass of shadow
would be moving—moving——

A noise, very slight, came from the library
behind the opened doors. The marine glasses
remained poised in the girl's hands while she
listened. Again the noise—a faint metallic
click.

She hardly breathed. Turning ever so slowly, she put one hand between the curtains and
parted them so that she could look through into
the cavernous gloom behind her.

A light moved there—a clear round eye of
light. Behind it was the faintest suggestion of

a figure at the double doors—just a blur of white, it was; but it moved stealthily, swiftly. She heard a key turn in a lock. Then swiftly the eye of light traveled across the library to the door leading to General Crandall's room. There it paused to cut the handle of the door and keyhole beneath out of darkness. A brown hand slipped into the clear shaft of whiteness, put a key into the keyhole, and softly turned it. The same was done for the locks of Lady Crandall's door, on the opposite side of the library, and for the one Jane had just closed behind her —her own door. Then the circle of light, seeming to have an intelligence all its own, approached the desk, flew swiftly to a drawer and there paused. Once more the brown hand plunged into the bore of light; the drawer was carefully opened, and a steel-blue revolver reflected bright sparks from its barrel as it was withdrawn.

Jane, hardly daring to breathe, and with the heavy curtains gathered close so that only a space for her eyes was left open, watched the orb of light, fascinated. It groped under the desk, found a nest of slender wires. There was a "Snick—snick!" and the severed ends of the wires dropped to the floor. The burnished dial of the wall safe, set near the double doors, was the next object to come under the restless searching eye. While light poured steadily upon the circular bit of steel, delicate fingers played with it, twisting and turning this way and that. Then they were laid upon the handle of the safe door, and it swung noiselessly back. A tapering brown hand, white-sleeved, fumbled in a small drawer, withdrew a packet of papers and selected one.

Jane stepped boldly into the room.

"Sahibah!" The white club of the electric flash smote her full in the face.

"What are you doing at that safe, Jaimihr Khan?" Jane spoke as steadily as she could, though excitement had its fingers at her throat, and all her nerves were twittering. She heard some sharply whistled foreign word, which might have been a curse.

"Something that concerns you not at all, Sahibah," the Indian answerd, his voice smooth as oil. He kept the light fair on her face.

"I intend that it shall concern me," the girl answered, taking a step forward.

"Veree, veree foolish, Sahibah!" Jaimihr whispered, and with catlike stride he advanced to meet her. "Veree foolish to come here at this time."

Jane, frozen with horror at the man's approach, dodged and ran swiftly to the fireplace, where hung the ancient vesper bell. The flash light followed her every move—picked out her hand as it swooped down to seize a heavy poker standing in its rack beside the bell.

"Sahibah! Do not strike that bell!" The warning came sharp and cold as frost. Her hand was poised over the bell, the heavy stub of the poker a very few inches away from the bell's flare.

"To strike that bell might involve in great trouble one who is veree dear to you, Sahibah. Let us talk this over most calmly. Surely you would not desire that a friend—a veree dear friend——"

"Who do you mean?" she asked sharply.

"Ah—that I leave to you to guess!" Jaimihr Khan's voice was silken. "But certainly you know, Sahibah. A friend the most important——"

Then she suddenly understood. The Indian

was referring to Captain Woodhouse thus glibly. Anger blazed in her.

"It isn't true!"

"Sahibah, I am sorry to con-tradict." Jai-mihr Khan had begun slowly to creep toward her, his body crouching slightly as a stalking cat's.

"I'll prove it isn't true!" she cried, and brought the poker down on the bell with a sharp blow. Like a tocsin came its answering alarm.

"A thousand devils!" The Indian leaped for the girl, but she evaded him and ran to put the desk between herself and him. He had snapped off the torch at the clang of the bell, and now he was a pale ghost in the gloom—fearsome. Hissing Indian curses, he started to circle the desk to seize her.

"Open this door! Open it, I say!" It was the general's voice, sounding muffled through the panels of his door; he rattled the knob viciously. Jane tried to run to the door, but the Indian seized her from behind, threw her aside, and made for the double doors. There his hand went to a panel in the wall, turned a light switch, and the library was on the in-

stant drenched with light. Jaimihr Khan
threw before the door of the safe the bundle
of papers he was clutching when Jane discovered him and which he had gripped during the
ensuing tense moments. Then he stepped
swiftly to the general's door and unlocked it.

General Crandall, clad only in trousers and
shirt, burst into the room. His eyes leaped
from the Indian to where Jane was cowering
behind his desk.

"What the devil is this?" he rasped.   Jane
opened her mouth to answer, but the Indian
forestalled her:

"The sahibah, General—I found her here before your opened safe——"

"Good God!" General Crandall's eyes blazed.
He leaped to the safe, knelt and peered in.   "A
clever job, young woman!"

Jane, completely stunned by the Indian's
swift strategy, could hardly speak.   She held
up a hand, appealing for a hearing.   General
Crandall eyed her with chilling scorn, then
turned to his servant.

"You have done well, Jaimihr."

"It—it isn't true!" Jane stammered.   The
governor took a step toward her almost as if

under impulse to strike her, but he halted, and his lips curled in scorn.

"By gad, working with Woodhouse all the time, eh? And I thought you a simple young woman he had trapped—even warned you against him not six hours ago. What a fool I've been!" Jane impulsively stretched forth her arms for the mercy of a hearing, but the man went on implacably:

"I said he was making a fool of you—and all the time you were making one of me. Clever young woman. I say, that must have been a great joke for you—making a fool of the governor of Gibraltar. You make me ashamed of myself. And my servant—Jaimihr here; it is left to him to trap you while I am blind. Bah! Jaimihr, my orderly—at once!" The Indian smiled sedately and started for the double doors. Jane ran toward the general with a sharp cry:

"General—let me explain——"

"Explain!" He laughed shortly. "What can you say? You come into my house as a friend— you betray me—you break into my safe—with Woodhouse, whom I'd warned you against, directing your every move. Clever—clever! Jaimihr, do as I tell you. My orderly at once!"

Jane threw herself between the Indian and the doors.

"One moment—before he leaves the room let me tell you he lies? Your Indian lies. It was I who found him here—before that safe!"

"A poor story," the general sniffed. "I expected better of you—after this."

"The truth, General Crandall. I couldn't sleep. I came out here to the balcony to try to make out if the *Saxonia* was in the bay. He came into the room while I was behind these curtains, locked the doors, and opened the safe."

"It won't go," the general cut in curtly.

"It's the truth—it's got to go!" she cried.

Jaimihr, at a second nod from his master, was approaching the double doors. Jane, leaping in front of them, pushed the Indian back.

"General Crandall, for your own sake—don't let this Indian leave the room. You may regret it—all the rest of your life. He still has a paper —a little paper—he took from that safe. I saw him stick it in his sash."

"Nonsense!"

"Search him!" The girl's voice cracked in hysteria; her face was dead white, with hectic burning spots in each cheek. "I'm not pleading for myself now—for you. Search him before he leaves this room!"

Jaimihr put strong hands on her arms to force her away from the door. His black eyes were laughing down into hers.

"Let me ask him a question first, General Crandall—before he leaves this room."

The governor's face reflected momentary surprise at this change of tack. "Quickly then," he gruffly conceded. Jaimihr Khan stepped back a pace, his eyes meeting the girl's coldly.

"How did you come into the room—when you found me here?" she challenged. The Indian pointed to the double doors over her shoulder. She reached behind her, grasped the knob, and shook it. "Locked!" she announced.

"Why not?" Jaimihr asked. "I locked them after me."

"And the general's door was locked?"

"Yes—yes!" Crandall broke in impatiently. "What's this got to do with——"

"Did you lock the general's door?" she questioned the Indian.

"No, Sahibah; you did."

"And I suppose I locked the door to Lady Crandall's room and my door?"

"If they, too, are locked—yes, Sahibah."

"Then why"—Jane's voice quavered almost to a shriek—"why had I failed to lock the double doors—the doors through which you came?"

The Indian caught his breath, and darted a look at the general. The latter, eying him keenly, stepped to his desk and pressed a button.

"Very good; remain here, Jaimihr," he said. Then to Jane: "I will have him searched, as you wish. Then both of you go to the cells until I sift this thing to the bottom."

"General! You wouldn't dare!" She stood aghast.

"Wouldn't I, though? We'll see whether—" A sharp click sent his head jerking around to the right. Jaimihr Khan, at the door to the general's room, was just slipping the key into his girdle, after having turned the lock. His thin face was crinkled like old sheepskin.

"What the devil are you doing?" Crandall exploded.

"If the general sahib is waiting for that bell

to be answered—he need not wait longer—it will not be answered," Jaimihr Khan purred.

"What's this—what's this!"

"The wires are cut."

"Cut! Who did that?" The general started for the yellow man. Jaimihr Khan whipped a blue-barreled revolver out of his broad sash and leveled it at his master.

"Back, General Sahib! I cut them. The sahibah's story is true. It was she who came in and found me at the safe."

"My God! You, Jaimihr—you a spy!" The general collapsed weakly into a chair by the desk.

"Some might call me that, my General." Jaimihr's weapon was slowly swinging to cover both the seated man and the girl by the doors. "No need to search that drawer, General Sahib. Your pistol is pointing at you this minute."

"You'll pay for this!" Crandall gasped.

"That may be. One thing I ask you to remember. If one of you makes a move I will kill you both. You are a gallant man, my General; is it not so? Then remember."

Crandall started from his chair, but the uselessness of his bare hands against the snub-

nosed thing of blue metal covering him struck
home. He sank back with a groan. Keeping
them both carefully covered, Jaimihr moved to
the desk telephone at the general's elbow. He
took from his sash a small piece of paper—the
one he had saved from the packet of papers
taken from the safe—laid it on the edge of the
desk, and with his left hand he picked up the
telephone. An instant of tense silence, broken
by the wheezing of the general's breath,
then——

"Nine-two-six, if you please. Yes—yes, who
is this? Ah, yes. It is I, Jaimihr Khan. Is all
well with you? Good! And Bishop? Slain
coming down the Rock—good also!"

Crandall groaned. The Indian continued his
conversation imperturbed.

"Veree good! Listen closely. I can not come
as I have promised. There is—work—for me
here. But all will be well. Take down what I
shall tell you." He read from the slip of paper
on the desk. "Seven turns to the right, four to
the left—press! Two more to the left—press!
One to the right. You have that? Allah speed
you. Go quickly!"

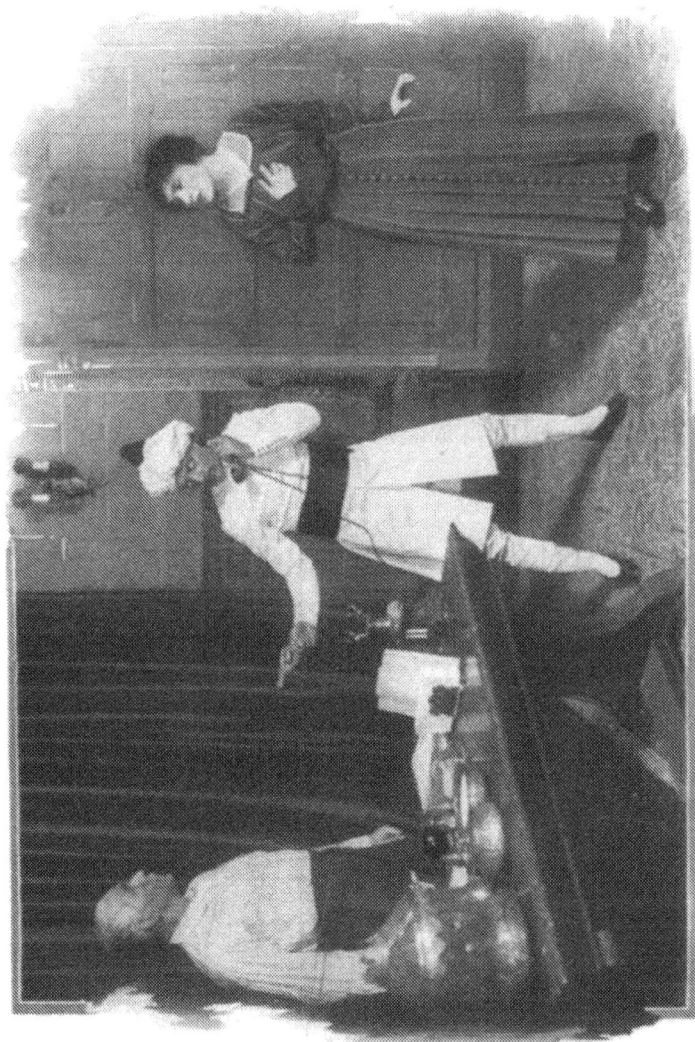

"There is—work—for me here."

"Room D!" Crandall had leaped from his chair.

"Correct, my General—Room D." Jaimihr smiled as he stepped away from the telephone, his back against the double doors. The sweat stood white on Crandall's brow; his mouth worked in jerky spasms.

"What—what have you done?" he gasped.

"I see the general knows too well," came the Indian's silken response. "I have given the combination of the inner door of Room D in the signal tower to a—friend. He is on his way to the tower. He will be admitted—one of the few men on the Rock who could be admitted at this hour, my General. One pull of the switches in Room D—and where will England's great fleet be then?"

"You yellow devil!" Crandall started to rush the white figure by the doors, but his flesh quailed as the round cold muzzle met it. He staggered back.

"We are going to wait, my General—and you, American Sahibah, who have pushed your way into this affair. We are going to wait—and listen—listen."

The general writhed in agony. Jane, fallen into a chair by the far edge of the desk, had her head buried in her arms, and was sobbing.

"And we are going to think, my General," the Indian's voice purled on. "While we wait we shall think. Who will General Crandall be after to-night—the English sahib who ruled the Rock the night the English fleet was blown to hell from inside the fortress? How many widows will curse when they hear his name? What——"

"Jaimihr Khan, what have I ever done to you!" The governor's voice sounded hardly human. His face was blotched and purple.

"Not what you have done, my General—what the English army has done. An old score, General—thirty years old. My father—he was a prince in India—until this English army took away his throne to give it to a lying brother. The army—the English army—murdered my father when he tried to get it back—called it mutiny. Ah, yes, an old score; but by the breath of Allah, to-night shall see it paid!"

The man's eyes were glittering points of white-hot steel. All of his thin white teeth showed like a hound's.

"You dog!" The general feebly wagged his head at the Indian.

"Your dog, my General. Five years your dog, when I might have been a prince. My friend goes up the Rock—step—step—step. Closer— closer to the tower, my General. And Major Bishop—where is he? Ah, a knife is swift and makes no noise——"

"What a fool I've been!" Crandall rocked in his chair, and passed a trembling hand before his eyes. Sudden rage turned his bloodshot eyes to where the girl was stretched, sobbing, across the desk. "Your man—the man you protected—it is he who goes to the signal tower, girl!"

"No—no; it can't be," she whispered between the rackings of her throat.

"It is! Only a member of the signal service could gain admittance into the tower to-night. Besides—who was it went with Bishop down the Rock after the dinner to-night? And I—I sent Bishop with him—sent him to his death. He was tricking you all the time. I told you he was. I warned you he was playing with you— using you for his own rotten ends—using you to help kill forty thousand men!"

It needed not the sledge-hammer blows of the stricken Crandall to batter Jane Gerson's heart. She had read too clearly the full story Jaimihr Khan's sketchy comments had outlined. She knew now Captain Woodhouse, spy. The Indian was talking again, his words dropping as molten metal upon their raw souls.

"Forty thousand men! A pleasant thought, my General. Eight minutes up the Rock to the tower when one moves fast. And my friend— ah, he moves veree—veree fast. Eight minutes, and four have already passed. Watch the windows—the windows looking out to the bay, General and Sahibah. They will flame—like blood. Your hearts will stop at the great noise, and then——"

A knock sounded at the double doors behind Jaimihr. He stopped short, startled. All listened. Again came the knock. Without turning his eyes from the two he guarded, Jaimihr asked: Who is it?"

"Woodhouse," came the answer.

Jane's heart stopped. Crandall sat frozen in his seat. Jaimihr turned the key in the lock, and the doors opened. In stepped Captain Woodhouse, helmeted, armed with sword and revolver at waist. He stood facing the trio, his swift eye taking in the situation at once. Crandall half rose from his seat, his face apoplectic.

"Spy! Secret killer of men!" he gasped.

Woodhouse paid no heed to him, but turned to Jaimihr.

"Quick! The combination," he said. "Over the phone—afraid I might not have it right—stopped here on my way to the tower—be there in less than three minutes if you can hold these people."

"Everything is all right?" Jaimihr asked suspiciously.

"You mean Bishop? Yes. Quick, the combination!"

Jaimihr picked the slip of paper containing the formula from the edge of the desk with his disengaged left hand and passed it to Woodhouse.

The latter stretched out his hand, grasped the Indian's with a lightning move, and threw it over so that the latter was off his balance. In a twinkling Woodhouse's left hand had wrenched the revolver from Jaimihr's right and pinioned it behind his back. The whole movement was accomplished in half a breath. Jaimihr Khan knelt in agony, and in peril of a broken wrist, at the white man's feet, disarmed, harmless. Woodhouse put a silver whistle to his lips and blew three short blasts.

A tramp of feet in the hallway outside, and four soldiers with guns filled the doorway.

"Take this man!" Woodhouse commanded.

The Indian, in a frenzy, writhed and shrieked:

"Traitor! English spy! Dog of an unbeliever!"

The soldiers jerked him to his feet and dragged him out; his ravings died away in the passage.

Woodhouse brought his hand up in a salute as he faced General Crandall.

"The other spy, Almer, of the Hotel Splendide, has just been arrested, sir. Major Bishop has taken charge of him and has lodged him in the cells."

A high-pitched scream sounded behind Lady Crandall's door, and a pounding on the panels. Jane Gerson, first to recover from the shock of surprise, ran to unlock the door. Lady Crandall, in a dressing gown, burst into the library and flung herself on her husband.

"George—George! What does all this mean
—yells—whistling——"

General Crandall gave his wife a pat on the
shoulder and put her aside with a mechanical
gesture. He took a step toward Woodhouse,
who still stood stiffly before the opened doors;
the dazed governor walked like a somnambulist.

"Who—who the devil are you, sir?" he managed to splutter.

"I am Captain Cavendish, General." Again
the hand came to stiff salute on the visor of the
pith helmet. "Captain Cavendish, of the signal
service, stationed at Khartum, but lately detached for special service under the intelligence
office in Downing Street."

The man's eyes jumped for an instant to seek
Jane Gerson's face—found a smile breaking
through the lines of doubt there.

"Your papers to prove your identity!" Crandall demanded, still in a fog of bewilderment.

"I haven't any, General Crandall," the other
replied, with a faint smile, "or your Indian, Jaimihr Khan, would have placed them in your
hands after the search of my room yesterday.
I've convinced Major Bishop of my genuineness,

however—after we left your house and when
the moment for action arrived. A cable to Sir
Ludlow-Service, in the Downing Street office,
will confirm my story. Meanwhile I am willing
to go under arrest if you think best."

"But—but I don't understand, Captain—er—
Cavendish. You posed as a German—as an
Englishman."

"Briefly, General, a girl secretly in the pay of
the Downing Street office—Louisa Schmidt,
—Josepha, the cigar girl, whom you ordered
locked up a few hours ago—is the English representative in the Wilhelmstrasse at Berlin.
She learned of a plan to get a German spy
in your signal tower a month before war was
declared, reported it to London, and I was
summoned from Khartum to London to play
the part of the German spy. At Berlin, where
she had gone from your own town of Gibraltar to meet me, she arranged to procure me a
number in the Wilhelmstrasse through the
agency of a dupe named Capper——"

"Capper! Good Lord!" Crandall stammered.

"With the number I hurried to Alexandria.
Woodhouse—Captain Woodhouse, from Wady

"Your prisoner, sir!"

Halfa—a victim, poor chap, to the necessities of our plan, fell into the hands of the Wilhelm-strasse men there, and I gained possession of his papers. The Germans started him in a rob-ber caravan of Bedouins for the desert, but I provided against his getting far before being rescued, and the German agents there were all rounded up the day I sailed as Woodhouse."

"And you came here to save Gibraltar—and the fleet from German spies?" Crandall put the question dazedly.

"There were only two, General—Almer and your servant, Jaimihr. We have them now. You may order the release of Louisa Schmidt."

"The captain has overlooked one other—the most dangerous one of all, General Crandall." Jane stepped up to where the governor stood and threw back her hands with an air of sub-mission. "Her name is Jane Gerson, of New York, and she knew all along that this gentle-man was deceiving you—she had met him, in fact, three weeks before on a railroad train in France."

The startled eyes of Gibraltar's master looked first at the set features of the man, then to the girl's flushed face. Little lines of humor crinkled about the corners of his mouth.

"Captain Cavendish—or Woodhouse, make this girl a prisoner—your prisoner, sir!"

CHAPTER XIX

FIVE o'clock at the quay, and already the new day was being made raucous by the bustle of departure—shouts of porters, tenders' jangling engine bells, thump of trunks dropped down skidways, lamentations of voyagers vainly hunting baggage mislaid. Out in the stream the *Saxonia*—a clean white ship, veritable ark of refuge for pious Americans escaping the deluge.

In the midst of a group of his countrymen Henry J. Sherman stood, feet wide apart and straw hat cocked back over his bald spot. He was narrating the breathless incidents of the night's dark hour:

"Yes, sir, a soldier comes to our rooms about three-thirty o'clock and hammers on our door. 'Everybody in this hotel's under arrest,' he says. 'Kindly dress as soon as possible and report to Major Bishop in the office.' And we not five hours before the guests of General and Lady Crandall at Government House. What d'you think of that for a quick change?

"Well, gentlemen, we piled down-stairs—with me minus a collar button and havin' to hold my collar down behind with my hand. And what do we find? This chap Almer, with a face like a side of cream cheese, standing in the middle of a bunch of soldiers with guns; another bunch of soldiers surroundin' his Arab boy, who's as innocent a little fellah as ever you set eyes on; and this Major Bishop walkin' up and down, all excited, and sayin' something about somebody's got a scheme to blow up the whole fleet out there. Which might have been done, he says, if it wasn't for that fellah Woodhouse we'd had dinner with just that very evening."

"Who's some sort of a spy. I knew it all the time, you see." Mrs. Sherman was quick to claim her share of her fellow tourists' attention. "Only he's a British spy set to watch the Germans. Major Bishop told me that in confidence after it was all over—said he'd never met a man with the nerve this Captain Woodhouse has."

"Better whisper that word 'spy' soft," Henry J. admonished sotto voce. "We're not out of this plagued Europe yet, and we've had about all the excitement we can stand; don't want anybody to arrest us again just the minute we're sailin'. But, as I was sayin', there we all stood, foolish as goats, until in comes General Crandall, followed by this Woodhouse chap. 'Excuse me, people, for causing you this little inconvenience,' the general says. 'Major Bishop has taken his orders too literal. If you'll go back to your rooms and finish dressin' I'll have the army bus down here to take you to the quay. The Hotel Splendide's accommodations have been slightly disarranged by the arrest of its worthy proprietor.' So back we go, and—by cricky, mother, here comes the general and Mrs. Crandall now!"

Henry J. broke through the ring of passengers, and with a waving of his hat, rushed to the curb. A limousine bearing the governor, his lady and Jane Gerson, and with two bulky hampers strapped to the baggage rack behind, was just drawing up.

"Why, of course we're down here to see you

off—and bid you Godspeed to little old Kewanee!" Lady Crandall was quick to antici-
pate the Shermans' greetings. General Crandall, beaming indulgently on the group of
homegoers, had a hand for each.

"Yes—yes," he exclaimed. "After arresting
you at three o'clock we're here to give you a
clean ticket at five. Couldn't do more than that
—what? Regrettable occurrence and all that,
but give you something to tell the stay-at-
homes about when you get back to—ah——"

"Kewanee, Illynoy, General," Sherman was
quick to supply. "No town like it this side the
pearly gates."

"No doubt of it, Sherman," Crandall heartily
agreed. "A quiet place, I'll wager. Think I'd
relish a touch of your Kewanee after—ah—life
on Gibraltar."

Jane Gerson, who had been standing in the
car, anxiously scanning the milling crowd about
the landing stage, caught sight of a white helmet and khaki-clad shoulders pushing through
the nearer fringes of travelers. She slipped
out of the limousine unseen, and waited for the
white helmet to be doffed before her.

"I was afraid maybe——" the girl began her cheeks suddenly flaming.

"Afraid that, after all, it wasn't true?" the man she had found in war's vortex finished, his gray eyes compelling hers to tell him their whole message. "Afraid that Captain Cavendish might be as vile a deceiver as Woodhouse? Does Cavendish have to prove himself all over again, little girl?"

"No—no!" Her hands fluttered into his, and her lips were parted in a smile. "It's Captain Woodhouse I want to know—always; the man whose pledged word I held to."

"It must have been—hard," he murmured. "But you were splendid—splendid!"

"No, I was not." Tears came to dim her eyes, and the hands he held trembled. "Once —in one terrible moment this morning—when Jaimihr told us you were going to the signal tower—when we waited—waited to hear that awful noise, my faith failed me. I thought you——"

"Forget that moment, Jane, dearest. A saint would have denied faith then."

They were silent for a minute, their hearts

quailing before the imminent separation.   He
spoke:

"Go back to the States now; go back and
show this Hildebrand person you're a wonder
—a prize.   Show him what I've known more
and more surely every moment since that meeting in Calais.   But give him fair warning; he's
going to lose you."

"Lose me?" she echoed.

"Inevitably.   Listen, girl!   In a year my
term of service is up, and if the war's over I
shall leave the army, come to the States to you,
and—and—do you think I could become a good
American?"

"If—if you have the proper teacher," the
girl answered, with a flash of mischief.

"All aboard for the *Saxonia!*"   It was Consul Reynolds, fussed, perspiring, overwhelmed
with the sense of his duty, who bustled up to
where the Shermans were chatting with Lady
Crandall and the general.   Reynolds' sharp eye
caught an intimate tableau on the other side
of the auto.   "And that means you, Miss Step-
lively New York," he shouted, "much as I hate
to—ah—interrupt."

Jane Gerson saw her two precious hampers

stemming a way through the crowd on the backs of porters, bound for the tender's deck. She could not let them out of her sight.

"Wait, Jane!" His hands were on her arms, and he would not let her go. "Will you be my teacher? I want no other."

"My terms are high." She tried to smile, though trembling lips belied her.

"I'd pay with my life," he whispered in a quick gust of passion. "Here's my promise——"

He took her in his arms, and between them passed the world-old pledge of man and girl.

THE END

www.ingramcontent.com/pod-product-compliance
Lightning Source LLC
Chambersburg PA
CBHW021215090426
42740CB00006B/227